Brush Up Your Shakespeare!

MICHAEL MACRONE

ILLUSTRATIONS BY TOM LULEVITCH

PAVILION

First published in Great Britain in 1993 by
PAVILION BOOKS LIMITED
26 Upper Ground, London SE1 9PD

Text copyright © Cader Company, Inc. 1991
Illustrations © Tom Lulevitch 1991

Verse from 'Brush Up Your Shakespeare' © 1976 by Cole Porter
and Buxton-Hill-Music Corporation. Administered by Chappell
and Co. All rights reserved. Used by permission.

Created by Cader Books, New York

Published by arrangement with
HarperCollins Publishers, New York

A CIP catalogue record for this book is available from the
British Library

ISBN 1 85793 103 3

Printed and bound in Great Britain by
WBC, Bridgend, Mid Glam.

4 6 8 10 9 7 5

Brush Up
Your Shakespeare!

Contents

List of Illustrations

Acknowledgments

Selections from Shakespeare's plays and poems are based on the texts prepared by G. Blakemore Evans for *The Riverside Shakespeare* (Houghton Mifflin), which is the best single-volume American edition of Shakepeare's works. Act, scene, and line numbers uniformly refer to this edition. I have, however, taken the liberty of an independent collation and have occasionally introduced readings and punctuation from other editions.

In documenting occurrence and usage of words and phrases, I have relied on a number of works, a few of which deserve special mention. The second edition of the *Oxford English Dictionary* (1989)—abbreviated *OED*—serves as the first authority, although in matters of first occurrence it is sometimes superseded. Jürgen Schäfer's *Documentation in the O.E.D.: Shakespeare and Nashe as Test Cases* (Oxford, 1980) was invaluable in compiling the list in this book entitled "Household Words"—Schäfer documents occurrences predating those even in the subsequent *OED* of 1989. C. T. Onions's *A Shakespeare Glossary* (2nd ed., Oxford, 1922), deriving from the first edition of the *OED*, was the primary source for the first compilation of these occurrences.

My authorities in matters of proverbial speech are primarily two: *The Oxford Dictionary of English Proverbs*, edited by F. P. Wilson (3rd ed., Oxford, 1970) and R. W. Dent's *Shakespeare's Proverbial Language: An Index* (Berkeley, 1981). Recognizing that a proverb is often in the eye of the beholder, I have been slightly more liberal than Dent in allowing Shakespeare the invention of certain phrases.

All these texts have been essential to the composition of this book, but human beings have also played a role. I should like to thank Michael Cader of Cader Books first and foremost; without him this book would not exist. From conception to finished manuscript, he has been a generous and dedicated accomplice. I should also like to thank Nellie Haddad, who helped me collate editions of the plays and who offered equally generous support at every step in the writing process. Finally, I wish to thank Hugh Van Dusen, my editor at Harper & Row.

On behalf of Cader Books, thanks for steadfast guidance and support during the publishing process are also owed to Renee Schwartz, Patty Brown, and Rona and Arthur Rosenbaum, and to Kenneth Greif who, through his marvelous instruction, inadvertently inspired this book.

MICHAEL MACRONE

At First Brush

Brush up your Shakespeare,
Start quoting him now—
Brush up your Shakespeare
And the women you will wow.

Cole Porter, "Brush Up Your Shakespeare"

Cole Porter recommended this technique in the 1940s, but by then his advice was hardly necessary. Whether they knew it or not, people had been quoting Shakespeare piecemeal for hundreds of years. Indeed, we have derived from Shakespeare's works an almost "infinite variety" [*Antony and Cleopatra*] of everyday words and phrases, many of which have become so common that we think of them as "household words" [*Henry the Fifth*].

"Neither a borrower nor a lender be," counsels Polonius in *Hamlet*, but his famous advice is definitely (to quote the prince of Denmark out of context) "more honored in the breach than the observance." Our borrowings flow "trippingly on the tongue" (*Hamlet* again), usually without much thought of their original source to get in the way. Sometimes we intend to quote Shakespeare and want everyone to know it, but too often we give him "short shrift" [*Richard the Third*].

According to the man who invented the phrase, "short shrift" isn't something you can "give" at all (it's a hasty confession, something made rather than given). In other words, we quote the Bard "not wisely but too well" [*Othello*], observing the letter and violating the spirit. So "there's the rub" [*Hamlet*] —even when we know where we got the words, we don't always know what they really mean. ("Rub," for instance, is a piece of bowling terminology—and the Bard was a big bowler.)

So before you start quoting Shakespeare—or rather, before you continue quoting Shakespeare—you might want to do a little brushing up. (And if you've ever wondered whether high school students are mature enough to learn about a "bare bodkin," read on.) We're here to give you a handle on the famous lines you already know are Shakespeare's, and to alert you to our quieter, less conspicuous borrowings, those we appropriate without "pomp and circumstance" [*Othello*]. In the meantime, you'll be offered an incidental introduction (or reintroduction) to famous passages, concisely explained—after all, "brevity is the soul of wit" [*Hamlet*]—allowing you to master a pretty piece of Shakespeare while freeing you from the necessity of reading all the originals.

Organization

The main entries are arranged alphabetically by the first word in each phrase that the reader is likely to remember. Thus, "He hath eaten me out of house and home" is alphabetized by "eaten," and "To thine own self be true" by "to." If you have trouble finding a favorite line, check the index, where I've attempted to cross-list entries by all the key words.

Phrases include both famous lines and everyday expressions not normally associated with Shakespeare. In the case of the latter, I've tried my best to determine that Shakespeare's is the first recorded use, and I've availed myself of the most recent scholarship. In several cases, however—for example, "wild-goose chase," "cruel to be kind," and "good riddance"—it seems likely that the phrase had appeared in spoken English before Shakespeare set it down. It's ultimately a happy accident that Shakespeare's works are so well preserved, especially since drama was not an esteemed medium in his time. In the echo chamber of the history of English, it's often impossible to tell where phrases and proverbs originate. And in an oral culture, linguistic invention is rarely the work of any particular author.

The phrases I've included, however, may be laid at Shakespeare's door (even if by default) with some confidence. On the other hand, there are some expressions regularly attributed to the Bard that, upon further research, turn out to be proverbial or preserved in earlier writings. Though Shakespeare may have popularized (however indirectly) such phrases as "it's Greek to me" and "all that glitters is not gold," they're unfortunately not his inventions. I advise you, then, to consult the "Faux Shakespeare" section of this book to avoid embarrassment, in case you're writing a story of English or trying to look literary.

Each entry in the main section comprises an epigraph selection from the original text and a short commentary. I've endeavored to keep the epigraph as short as possible, for simplicity's sake, while still providing enough of the context to make the key phrase intelligible. Frankly, though, even on the page, let alone the stage, Shakespeare's English can be difficult to follow, so I've tried to spell out the salient details and gloss the obscurities. The rest of my remarks generally concern the origins or implications of the key phrase and are intended as guideposts rather than exhaustive explications.

A good number of phrases are cross-referenced when other entries provide helpful context or interesting sidelights. Cross-references are set in small capitals. If the cross reference is to a phrase directly quoted in the text, I simply supply the page number.

Included at the end of the main section is "Household Words," a survey of words invented by Shakespeare or, at the least, traced back no further than one of his plays. As with the phrases, I rely here on documentation sometimes at the expense of common sense. Shakespeare probably didn't, after all, invent the word "anchovy," but even the second edition of the *Oxford English Dictionary* (1989) can only trace the word back to *Henry the Fourth, Part 1*.

In the "Good Enough to Call Your Own" section of this book, I survey a few (just a few) book and article titles borrowed from the Bard and supply dates of first publication and the title's source in Shakespeare's canon.

Spelling and Punctuation

In the epigraphs from the plays, I've only occasionally modernized spelling to a greater degree than does the editor of *The Riverside Shakespeare*. For the most part I've kept old spellings so as to preserve Shakespeare's way with words and sounds, and for the interest in the evolution of the language. If Shakespeare spells an important word in a confusing or obscure fashion, I decipher it in the subsequent text.

Especially important in preserving at least the rhythm if not the exact sound of the original is the treatment of past participles—verb forms that end in *-ed*. When an apostrophe and *d* (*-'d*) are used to end a word in the epigraph, the *e* of *-ed* is silent—just as in modern English. Whenever *-ed* is spelled out, the *e* is pronounced; in these cases, I've added a redundant accent (*-èd*) as a reminder. Thus, "pleas'd" is pronounced just as we pronounce it today, as a one-syllable word; "pleasèd," however, is a two-syllable word with the accent on the first syllable.

Most other uses of the apostrophe indicate similar elisions of unpronounced vowels. When I'm not directly quoting Shakespeare, however—for example, in the phrase headings—I spell out the word as it is spelled today. Some apostrophes serve a different function; editors supply them to mark a word as a contraction or as a dialect pronunciation. The most frequent such contractions are *"a' "* for "he" or "she"; *"an' "* for "if" (that is, for "and," which is a short form of the phrase "and if"); *"i' th' "* for "in the"; and *"o' th' "* for "of the."

In my text, I've used the virgule (/) to mark the break between lines of quoted verse. Epigraphs themselves are set so as to distinguish verse passages from prose passages: verse is indented uniformly to the right of the speech prefix (which identifies the speaker), and the right margin is ragged. Prose wraps back below the speech prefix. When a second (or third) speaker continues a verse line begun by the first speaker, his or her speech will be marked by the appropriate indentation.

Dating

William Shakespeare (1564–1616) wrote at least 36 plays, 154 sonnets, and 4 longer poems. He wrote the better part of another play—*Henry the Eighth*—and a number of scenes of the Chaucerian *Two Noble Kinsmen*; both plays are, from all evidence, collaborations with the younger playwright John Fletcher. Shakespeare is believed to have contributed to a play called *Sir Thomas More*, and he may also have written two plays now lost: *Love's Labor's Won* and *Cardenio*. Even more tentative than *what* plays Shakespeare wrote is *when* they were written. In most cases, reliable testimony is lacking, so scholars have to go with their best guess.

All this matters here only because dating the plays is crucial in determining whether a word or phrase first appears in Shakespeare. There is many a case of an occurrence of a Bardism within striking distance of Shakespeare's alleged invention. To be on the safe side, I have opted for the more conservative datings by recent editors and have abandoned the frequently earlier datings of the *OED*. If you're interested, here is the chronological sequence of Shakespeare's plays and poems, as determined by G. Blakemore Evans in *The Riverside Shakespeare*:

King Henry the Sixth, Part 1	1589–90; revised 1594–95
King Henry the Sixth, Part 2	1590–91
King Henry the Sixth, Part 3	1590–91
King Richard the Third	1592–93
Venus and Adonis [poem]	1592–93
The Comedy of Errors	1592–94
Sonnets [poems]	1593–99
A Lover's Complaint [poem]	? (published 1609)
The Rape of Lucrece [poem]	1593–94
Titus Andronicus	1593–94
The Taming of the Shrew	1593–94
The Two Gentlemen of Verona	1594
Love's Labor's Lost	1594–95; revised 1597
King John	1594–96
King Richard the Second	1595
Romeo and Juliet	1595–96
A Midsummer Night's Dream	1595–96
The Merchant of Venice	1596–97
King Henry the Fourth, Part 1	1596–97
The Merry Wives of Windsor	1597; revised ca. 1600

King Henry the Fourth, Part 2	1598
Much Ado about Nothing	1598–99
King Henry the Fifth	1599
Julius Caesar	1599
As You Like It	1599
Hamlet	1600–1
The Phoenix and the Turtle [poem]	ca. 1601
Twelfth Night	1601–2
Troilus and Cressida	1601–2
All's Well that Ends Well	1602–3
Measure for Measure	1604
Othello	1604
King Lear	1605
Macbeth	1606
Antony and Cleopatra	1606–7
Coriolanus	1607–8
Timon of Athens	1607–8
Pericles, Prince of Tyre	1607–8
Cymbeline	1609–10
The Winter's Tale	1610–11
The Tempest	1611
King Henry the Eighth	1612–13
The Two Noble Kinsmen	1613

Brush Up
Your Shakespeare!

The Quotable and the Notable:
FAMOUS PHRASES FROM SHAKESPEARE

All the World's a Stage

JAQUES: All the world's a stage,
            And all the men and women merely players;
            They have their exits and their entrances,
            And one man in his time plays many parts,
            His acts being seven ages.

AS YOU LIKE IT   Act 2, scene 7, 139–143

The idea that "all the world's a stage" was already clichéd when Shakespeare wrote *As You Like It*. So Jaques is intended to sound at least a little pretentious here. Jaques (pronounced "jay-keys" or "jay-kweez") is the resident sourpuss in the Forest of Arden, home to political exiles, banished lovers, and simple shepherds. Picking up on another character's stray suggestion that the world is a "wide and universal theater," Jaques deploys the theatrical metaphor for his famous speech on the Seven Ages of Man. The first of these ages, according to Jaques, is

infancy (when the babe is found "Mewling [sobbing] and puking in his nurse's arms"), and the last is "second childishness and mere oblivion" (complete senility). His glum epigrams make up a "set speech"; Shakespeare meant them to sound practiced, like a bit of oratory polished off and hauled out on the appropriate (or inappropriate) occasion.

Antic Disposition

HAMLET: But come—
        Here, as before, never, so help you mercy,
        How strange or odd some'er I bear myself—
        As I perchance hereafter shall think meet
        To put an antic disposition on—
        That you, at such times seeing me, never shall,
        With arms encumb'red thus, or this headshake,
        Or by pronouncing of some doubtful phrase,

As "Well, well, we know," or "We could, and if we would,"
Or "If we list to speak," or "There be, and if they might,"
Or such ambiguous giving out, to note
That you know aught of me—this do swear,
So grace and mercy at your most need help you.

HAMLET   Act 1, scene 5, 168–180

We use "antic" as a synonym of "madcap," stressing deliberate playfulness. But for most of its history the word referred to grotesque and ludicrous qualities, especially in drama and pageants. With a sort of ironic understatement, Hamlet uses "antic" not to mean "madcap," exactly, but something closer to "mad"—bizarre, irrational, threatening.

How theatrical Hamlet's "antic disposition" will eventually prove is the subject of much debate. At times, it seems that the prince has stopped playing a part and has in fact *become* antic. Hamlet's performance will be all too plausible; but then again, he's been a student of the theater and is no mere amateur [see THE GLASS OF FASHION].

This scene comes at the end of Hamlet's first meeting with his father's ghost; he is swearing his friend Horatio and the officer Marcellus to secrecy about plans he hasn't really explained [see THERE ARE MORE THINGS IN HEAVEN AND EARTH, HORATIO]. Like the good actor he is, Hamlet plays out the coy gestures he'd have the two avoid—the kind of "ambiguous giving out" that would expose Hamlet's antic disposition as merely a clever charade.

Bated Breath

SHYLOCK: Go to then, you come to me, and you say,
"Shylock, we would have moneys," you say so. . . .
Shall I bend low and in a bondman's key,
With bated breath and whisp'ring humbleness,
Say this:
"Fair sir, you spet on me Wednesday last,
You spurn'd me such a day, another time
You call'd me dog; and for these courtesies
I'll lend you thus much moneys"?

THE MERCHANT OF VENICE Act 1, scene 3, 115–116, 123–129

The Venetian merchant Antonio and his friends take a dim view of Shylock, the Jewish usurer, and his practice of charging interest on loans. For his "un-Christian" behavior, the Christians spit on Shylock, call him a cur, and kick him around the streets of Venice. In this speech—delivered when, as was inevitable, Antonio calls on Shylock for a loan—the usurer turns Antonio's words and actions against him.

Shylock asks whether, after the treatment he's received, he should now servilely bow, whisper like a "bondman" (slave), and put himself at Antonio's disposal. He mocks the idea that he ought to respond "with bated breath"—a much misunderstood phrase. "To bate," like "to abate," means to diminish, reduce, or blunt. "With bated breath," therefore, means "in a hushed voice," with reduced "breath" (force of speech). We've adopted the phrase to mean, most often, "with one's breath held."

The Be-All and the End-All

MACBETH: If it were done, when 'tis done, then 'twere well
It were done quickly. If th' assassination
Could trammel up the consequence, and catch
With his surcease, success: that but this blow
Might be the be-all and the end-all—here,
But here, upon this bank and shoal of time,
We'd jump the life to come.

MACBETH   Act 1, scene 7, 1–7

Macbeth ponders assassinating King Duncan of Scotland, whose shoes he intends to fill [see CHANCE MAY CROWN ME]. If simply killing the king were all there was to it, he tells himself, there'd be no problem. But there are bound to be unpredictable and uncontrollable consequences, both in this life ("upon this bank and shoal of time") and in the "life to come." Yet he'd "jump" (risk) the spiritual penalties if he could be sure of immediate success here and now.

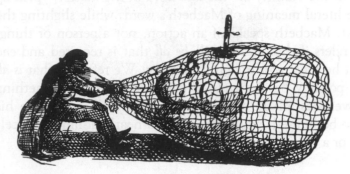

TRAMMEL UP THE CONSEQUENCE

"Trammel up the consequence" is ill understood, which hardly comes as a surprise. A "trammel," in Shakespeare's day, most often meant a "fishing net"; "to trammel up" therefore meant to catch up in a trammel net. (Another obsolete sense of "to trammel," current in the sixteenth century, is "to bind up a corpse"—a sense eerily appropriate here.) When Macbeth doubts whether the assassination could "trammel up the consequence," therefore, he doubts that the act of killing Duncan will catch up in itself, as in a net, the consequences of that action.

Macbeth, by the way, seems to have invented the word "assassination"—this is at least the first recorded use.

BE-ALL AND END-ALL

We use "the be-all and the end-all" in two rather different ways, neither of which pays much respect to Macbeth's intention. On one hand, the be-all and the end-all is something superlative in its category—a paragon or an extreme. On the other hand, the be-all and the end-all is an all-consuming project or passion—an *idée fixe*. Both uses, which meet somewhere in the vicinity of "the last word in the matter," pick up on the literal meaning of Macbeth's words while slighting the context. Macbeth speaks of an action, not a person or thing; he wonders if that action will *be all* that is required and *end all* that he must go through to be king. We refer to what *is all* it can possibly be and *ends all* competition, or to something that overrides all the normal limits. Macbeth would like his deed to be limited, while we admire a nearly unlimited excellence, or a passion without bounds.

To Beggar Description

ENOBARBUS: The barge she sat in, like a burnish'd throne,
　　　　　Burnt on the water. The poop was beaten gold,
　　　　　Purple the sails, and so perfumèd that
　　　　　The winds were love-sick with them; the oars were silver,
　　　　　Which to the tune of flutes kept stroke, and made
　　　　　The water which they beat to follow faster,
　　　　　As amorous of their strokes. For her own person,
　　　　　It beggar'd all description: she did lie
　　　　　In her pavilion—cloth of gold, of tissue—
　　　　　O'er-picturing that Venus where we see
　　　　　The fancy outwork nature.

ANTONY AND CLEOPATRA   **Act 2, scene 2, 191–201**

Marc Antony's friend Enobarbus describes Cleopatra as he and Antony first saw her, sailing in pageant down the river Cydnus.

While words might do justice to her barge, the queen herself "beggar'd all description." The verb "to beggar" dates only from the sixteenth century, and originally meant "to make a beggar of, to impoverish." In its figurative use here, "to beggar" means "to exhaust the resources of": to describe Cleopatra as she sailed by in her burnished throne is impossible because language is too poor.

On the other hand, Cleopatra does remind Enobarbus of a legendary painting of Venus. The artist's "fancy"—his imaginative power—renders a Venus more wonderful than anything in nature. Cleopatra does this portrait one better: she's a more spectacular work of art than even the most artful of paintings.

We Have Seen Better Days

DUKE SENIOR: True is it that we have seen better days,
And have with holy bell been knoll'd to church,
And sat at good men's feasts, and wip'd our eyes
Of drops that sacred pity hath engend'red;
And therefore sit you down in gentleness,
And take upon command what help we have
That to your wanting may be minst'red.

AS YOU LIKE IT   Act 2, scene 7, 120–126

When the hero of a romance chances upon a band of strangers in a dark and mysterious forest, he naturally assumes they're savages or criminals. Our hero Orlando is no exception, but this is a coterie of exiled courtiers, led by the deposed Duke Senior. The duke and his men have "seen better days," it is true, but they haven't forgotten their manners. Even as Orlando draws his sword and demands to be fed, the duke replies gently with a pitiful speech and freely offers help. From here on, all is well, but there are complications and surprises in store for everyone. Unbeknownst to either the Duke or Orlando, the woman our hero dotes on is the Duke's daughter.

'Tis Better to Be Vile than Vile Esteemed

> 'Tis better to be vile than vile esteemed,
> When not to be receives reproach of being,
> And the just pleasure lost, which is so deemed
> Not by our feeling, but by others' seeing.
> For why should others' false adulterate eyes
> Give salutation to my sportive blood?
>
> "Sonnet 121," 1–6

This is, frankly, one of my favorite passages in Shakespeare. The poet, in a complex sonnet full of ironies and paradoxes, challenges common notions of what is and is not "vile," and somewhat diabolically embraces as his good what the world thinks bad. " 'Tis better to be vile than vile esteemed" means "it's better to actually *be* 'bad' than to be *thought* bad." If what we do is judged "vile" not "by our feeling" but by the way others see things, then we may as well at least enjoy our pleasures, so long as not being vile invites the accusation anyway, without any of the attending pleasure. In other words, though the poet cares what other people think—he wouldn't complain if he didn't—he objects to their self-righteous condemnation of pleasures which seem "just" (innocent or proper) to him. These pleasures, clearly erotic, are part of what makes us human: they are a gift of nature, not a vile indulgence. The speaker concludes that if others think his lifestyle is vile, that says more about their imagination than his deeds.

"Sportive blood" is another phrase coined in this sonnet, and its sexual connotations should be apparent. Shakespeare often uses "blood" as a metaphor for passion, and "sportive" derives from a bawdy sense of "sport." "He had some feeling for the sport," Lucio confides in *Measure for Measure* (Act 3, scene 2), insinuating that the Duke was a womanizer. The speaker in this sonnet bristles at others' estimations of his own "sport"; "give salutation to" is a difficult phrase, perhaps meaning "judgmentally address themselves to."

The Better Part of Valor is Discretion

FALSTAFF: To die is to be a counterfeit, for he is but the counterfeit of
   a man who hath not the life of a man; but to counterfeit dying,
   when a man thereby liveth, is to be no counterfeit, but the true
   and perfect image of life indeed. The better part of valor is
   discretion, in the which better part I have sav'd my life.
                              HENRY THE FOURTH, PART 1   Act 5, scene 4, 115–121

Almost invariably quoted today as "Discretion is the better part of valor," Falstaff's phrase elegantly redeems a cowardly act. The bragging, bulbous knight has just risen from his feigned death; he had played the corpse in order to escape real death at the hands of a Scotsman hostile to Henry IV. Claiming that abstractions like "honor" and "valor" will get you nothing once you're dead, Falstaff excuses his counterfeiting as the kind of "discretion" that keeps a man from foolishly running into swords in order to cultivate a reputation for heroism. If counterfeiting keeps you alive, well then, it's not counterfeiting, but an authentic "image of life." Falstaff confuses "image" with "reality," but we forgive him; as far as he's concerned, "valor" is an image too, and you've got to stay alive in order to find more opportunities to cultivate that image.

Beware the Ides of March

CAESAR: Who is it in the press that calls on me?
           I hear a tongue shriller than all the music
           Cry "Caesar!" Speak, Caesar is turn'd to hear.
SOOTHSAYER: Beware the ides of March.
CAESAR: What man is that?
BRUTUS: A soothsayer bids you beware the ides of March.

JULIUS CAESAR Act 1, scene 2, 15–19

It is Lupercalia, an ancient Roman religious holiday. Caesar, the Roman dictator, makes his appearance before the "press" (crowd) in the streets. From out of the crowd, a soothsayer issues his famous warning. And Caesar, a very superstitious man, isn't the sort to take a soothsayer lightly.

The "ides" of March is the fifteenth; which day of the month the ides is depends on a complicated system of calculation Caesar himself established when he instituted the Julian calendar, a precursor of our own. The ides of January, for example, is the thirteenth; the ides of March, May, July and October is the fifteenth.

The importance of the ides of March for Caesar is that it is the day he will be assassinated by a group of conspirators, including Brutus and Cassius. Despite numerous and improbable portents—the soothsayer's warning, some fearsome thundering, his wife's dreams of his murder, and so on—Caesar ventures forth on the ides to meet his doom.

Shakespeare borrowed this scene, along with other details of Caesar's demise, from Plutarch's *Life of Julius Caesar.* An English translation was readily available, but its precise phrasings weren't quite dramatic enough for Shakespeare's purposes. Where he has the soothsayer declaim, "Beware the Ides of March," the more prosaic original notes merely that the soothsayer warns Caesar "to take heed of the day of the Ides of March."

A Blinking Idiot

ARRAGON: What's here? the portrait of a blinking idiot,
Presenting me a schedule! I will read it.
How much unlike art thou to Portia!
How much unlike my hopes and my deservings!
"Who chooseth me shall have as much as he deserves"!
Did I deserve no more than a fool's head?
Is that my prize? Are my deserts no better?

PORTIA: To offend and judge are distinct offices,
And of opposed natures.

THE MERCHANT OF VENICE Act 2, scene 9, 54–62

The beautiful, wealthy, and orphaned Portia has attracted the attention of a number of noble bachelors. But according to her father's will, she can give her hand in marriage only to the suitor who choses the one of three caskets which contains a small picture of the lady herself. Each casket is made of a different metal—gold, silver, or lead—and comes with an appropriate motto. The arrogant and appropriately named Prince of Arragon, responding to the motto "Who chooseth me shall have as much as he deserves," selects the silver casket, and finds therein a picture not of Portia, but of "a blinking idiot," a "fool's head," or dolt. When he protests that, surely, he deserves better than this, Portia replies stingingly that the offender is not an appropriate judge of his own case.

"Blinking" here can mean "winking," but there's no way what we mean by "blinking" could be represented in a picture. The idiot must be squinting his eyes, or have one open and one closed. In any case, it is sufficiently clear that the blockhead likened to Arragon has weak eyes, and therefore, metaphorically, weak perception. This judgment is reflected in our use of the phrase, even while we don't insist on any specific meaning at all for "blinking."

Brave New World

MIRANDA: O wonder!
How many goodly creatures are there here!
How beauteous mankind is! O brave new world
That has such people in't!

PROSPERO: 'Tis new to thee.

THE TEMPEST   Act 5, scene 1, 181–184

Exiled from Milan, the former duke Prospero and his admirable fifteen-year-old daughter Miranda have been stranded for twelve years on an uncharted isle in the Mediterranean. Miranda's entire experience of mankind has, until very recently, encompassed only her bitter old dad and his deformed slave Caliban [see THIS THING OF DARKNESS].

After reading up on white magic, Prospero succeeds in shipwrecking his old persecutors on the island and, after sufficiently humiliating them, produces them for his daughter's inspection. Miranda, trusting first impressions, finds these new "creatures" "goodly" and "brave." By "brave" she doesn't really mean "courageous," but rather "handsome" and "noble." Their wrecked ship had struck her as "brave"; her new fiancé Ferdinand looked pretty "brave" too; the whole pack of Italian princes and courtiers (most of them villains) are thus also "brave." Prospero has seen their inner workings, and knows how old this new world is, and how far from brave.

The phrase "brave new world" was your ordinary, not-terribly-quotable Shakespeareanism until Aldous Huxley put it on the map with his 1932 novel, *Brave New World.*

Breathe Life into a Stone

LAFEW: I have seen a medicine
       That's able to breathe life into a stone,
       Quicken a rock, and make you dance canary
       With spritely fire and motion, whose simple touch
       Is powerful to araise King Pippen, nay,
       To give great Charlemain a pen in 's hand
       And write to her a love-line.
                       ALL'S WELL THAT ENDS WELL   **Act 2, scene 1, 72–78**

The King of France, deathly ill, has been disappointed by so many supposed remedies that he's given up on medicine and despaired of recovery. The old lord Lafew, however, insists that there's one doctor who can save the king, the heroine of the play, Helena. Helena has inherited not only her father's

potent medicines, but an almost magical—even divine—healing power. Applying poetic images to convince the skeptical
king, Lafew claims that Helena's medicine can "breathe life
into a stone" and, synonymously, "Quicken a rock" (the images may derive from Genesis 2:7). Not content to stop there,
Lafew proclaims the medicine's power to make even an aged,
sickly king "dance canary" (canary is a particularly taxing
dance). The medicine—and the person of Helena—could, in
a pinch, raise Charlemagne's father Pepin from the grave, and
then Charlemagne himself. Helena never does quicken a rock,
nor does Charlemagne dash off any amorous notices, but she
does eventually cure the king.

Breathe One's Last

WARWICK: Come quickly, Montague, or I am dead.
SOMERSET: Ah, Warwick, Montague hath breath'd his last,
    And to the latest gasp cried out for Warwick,
    And said, "Commend me to my valiant brother."

HENRY THE SIXTH, PART 3 **Act 5, scene 2, 39–42**

When your library card "expires," what it's literally doing is "breathing out" its essence (that is, your borrowing privileges). When the Duke of Somerset reports that Warwick's brother Montague has "breathed his last," he's using "breathe" in this sense of "expire." Somerset leaves the phrase hanging, though: Montague has "breath'd his last" what? Elliptically, he means that Montague has drawn his last breath, or expired his last gasp. "Last gasp" is a phrase that entered the language about a decade before Shakespeare began writing, and he uses a version of the phrase—"latest gasp"—twice in this same play.

As the War of the Roses enters its penultimate act, hope seems lost for the Lancastrian faction, who support the weak King Henry VI. After a dizzying series of reversals for both the Lancastrians and Yorkists, the valiant Warwick, who has wreaked havoc on the forces of the usurper Edward IV, approaches his end, calling for help from his brother Montague. Somerset, who comes upon the wounded Warwick on the battlefield, is forced to report that Montague "hath breath'd his last," and with this news Warwick gives up the ghost.

Brevity Is the Soul of Wit

POLONIUS: My liege, and madam, to expostulate
What majesty should be, what duty is,
What day is day, night night, and time is time,
Were nothing but to waste night, day, and time;
Therefore, since brevity is the soul of wit,
And tediousness the limbs and outward flourishes,
I will be brief. Your noble son is mad. . . .

HAMLET Act 2, scene 2, 86–92

Polonius, right-hand man of Hamlet's stepfather, King Claudius, has been employed to spy on the prince and report on his very odd behavior. As Polonius begins to deliver to the king and queen the results of his investigation, he embarks on this windy preface. Besides being nonsensical, his speech is self-contradictory: he wastes plenty of time denouncing the time wasted by rhetorical speechifying.

"Brevity is the soul of wit" has become a standard English proverb; in the process, its context has been somewhat neglected. Polonius, though he has high opinions indeed of his "wit" (that is, acumen), is the least brief and one of the least "witty" characters in the play. Freud aptly referred to Polonius as "the old chatterbox" in *Jokes and their Relation to the Unconscious.*

Brief Authority

ISABELLA: Merciful heaven,
Thou rather with thy sharp and sulphurous bolt
Splits the unwedgeable and gnarlèd oak
Than the soft myrtle; but man, proud man,

Dress'd in a little brief authority,
Most ignorant of what he's most assur'd—
His glassy essence—like an angry ape
Plays such fantastic tricks before high heaven
As makes the angels weep; who, with our spleens,
Would all themselves laugh mortal.

MEASURE FOR MEASURE   Act 2, scene 2, 114–123

Isabella, a novice at the local convent, is pleading for her brother's life. Angelo, who's temporarily Vienna's chief executive, has got the idea into his head that it's up to him to reform the criminal justice system, and he begins by ruthlessly enforcing laws which had been ignored for years. One such law condemns fornicators to die, and Isabella's brother is the first victim. She has come to Angelo to beg for mercy—an essential quality of God's justice, as it ought thus be for man's justice.

As Angelo coldly refuses her entreaties, Isabella grows more passionate. She compares Heaven's tempering of its power to the cruel literalism of Angelo's justice. Heaven, when it strikes, at least strikes the most hardened and impassive victims —its thunder fells gnarled oaks, not soft myrtles. But Angelo, puffed up with pride by his "little brief authority"—his only temporary and limited power—arrogantly strikes out indiscriminately, even at soft myrtles like Isabella's young brother. Forgetting his "glassy essence"—the fragility of his soul, and its ultimate appointment with the Creator—arrogant man makes angels weep. If the angels had our "spleens" (self-regarding passions), they'd only laugh themselves to death.

Budge an Inch

HOSTESS: You will not pay for the glasses you have burst?
SLY: No, not a denier. Go by, Saint Jeronimy! go to thy cold bed, and
warm thee.
HOSTESS: I know my remedy; I must go fetch the thirdborough. [*Exit*]
SLY: Third, or fourth, or fifth borough, I'll answer him by law. I'll not
budge an inch, boy; let him come and kindly. [*Falls asleep*]

THE TAMING OF THE SHREW Induction, scene 1, 7–15

"I'll not budge an inch" is the greatest contribution the tinker Christopher Sly has made to everyday English. A version of the phrase—"I'll not yield an inch"—had entered the language not long before the composition of *The Taming of the Shrew*, but Sly's particular spin has endured. The use of "budge" as a verb, meaning "stir, move," was also very new; the earliest example we have is from 1590, about three years before Shakespeare's play.

As the *OED* points out, the verb has always been used almost exclusively in negative phrases—you will always "*not* budge" from somewhere; to say "Oh, sure, I'll budge if you like" sounds absurd. In another comedy written not long after *Shrew*, however, Launcelot Gobbo reports a contest between his good and bad consciences, the former saying "Launcelot, bouge not," while the latter urges him to "bouge" (*The Merchant of Venice*, Act 2, scene 2).

As *The Taming of the Shrew* opens, Sly stumbles drunkenly out of an alehouse, where he's been a rowdy fellow. When he spurns the hostess's demand that he pay for the glasses he's broken, she goes to fetch the law—the "thirdborough," or constable. His nonsensical response—"Go by, Saint Jeronimy!", etc.—mangles a famous line from Thomas Kyd's *The Spanish Tragedy* ("Go by, Hieronymo!"). Sly is one of those playgoing apprentices who, as London magistrates often complained, indulged in the corruptions of the theater and drunken carousing when they ought to have been tinkering at the shop.

Cakes and Ale

SIR TOBY: Art any more than a steward? Dost thou think because thou art virtuous there shall be no more cakes and ale?
FESTE: Yes, by Saint Anne, and ginger shall be hot i' th' mouth too.
SIR TOBY: Th' art i' th' right. Go, sir, rub your chain with crumbs. A stope of wine, Maria!
MALVOLIO: Mistress Mary, if you priz'd my lady's favor at any thing more than contempt, you would not give means for this uncivil rule. She shall know of it, by this hand.

TWELFTH NIGHT Act 2, scene 3, 114–124

While the Lady Olivia ostentatiously mourns her brother's death, her uncle Sir Toby Belch presides over late-night misrule in other quarters of her house. Olivia's dour, puritanical steward Malvolio gladly plays the law-enforcement officer, telling Toby and company, in effect, to cut the racket or pack off. Toby pulls rank on the steward, sarcastically demanding whether Malvolio thinks his "virtue" can be forced on everybody else, so that "there shall be no more cakes and ale." "Cakes and ale" is Toby's phrase for what Malvolio uncharitably calls "uncivil rule." This is the earliest recorded instance of the phrase, though "as good as cakes and pudding" predates *Twelfth Night.*

Americans understand a "cake" to be a fluffy confection preferably made with lots of chocolate and thickly layered with plenty of icing—not the sort of thing one normally serves with ale. The way Toby means it, however, a "cake" is merely a fancy or sweetened bread, which he classes with ale on the shopping list for the good life.

Caviar to the General

HAMLET: Come give us a taste of your quality, come, a passionate speech.

1ST PLAYER: What speech, my good lord?

HAMLET: I heard thee speak me a speech once, but it was never acted, or if it was, not above once; for the play, I remember, pleas'd not the million, 'twas caviare to the general. But it was, as I receiv'd it —and others, whose judgments in such matters cried in the top of mine—an excellent play, well digested in the scenes, set down with as much modesty as cunning.

HAMLET Act 2, scene 2, 431–440

"Caviar to the general" is not a delicacy prepared for the commanding officer. Like "pearls before swine," it refers to quality unbefitting those who partake in it. The "general" are the multitude—Hamlet's "million," too numerous and too vulgar to grasp the "quality" (here, "skill") of an excellent stage play.

Hamlet addresses the traveling dramatic troupe which has come to the Danish court to entertain the king. This is the same troupe the prince will use to "catch the conscience" of Claudius [see THE PLAY'S THE THING]. Hamlet nostalgically recalls a speech from a dramatization of the fall of Troy and commends the players' unappreciated skill. Shakespeare may be parodying the complaints of other playwrights, especially Ben Jonson, that the many-headed multitude don't know art when they see it. Despite Hamlet's Jonsonian snobbery, Shakespeare's own position was probably more ambivalent.

Chance May Crown Me

MACBETH: [Aside]   . . . Present fears
                Are less than horrible imaginings;
                My thought, whose murther yet is but fantastical,
                Shakes so my single state of man that function
                Is smother'd in surmise, and nothing is
                But what is not.
BANQUO: Look how our partner's rapt.
MACBETH: [Aside] If chance will have me king, why, chance may crown
                me
                Without my stir.

MACBETH   Act 1, scene 3, 137–144

No sooner do three witches proclaim Macbeth future king of Scotland than Macbeth starts thinking up bloody business. While his ambition gets ahead of his conscience, Macbeth is still frightened by his own "imaginings" of murdering the present king, Duncan (who's a relative, no less). The murder is as yet merely a fantasy ("fantastical"), but the fantasy is powerful enough to "smother" Macbeth's "function"—his normal grip on reality. For Macbeth, "nothing is/ But what is not": nothing is real to him but what is imaginary.

Macbeth's weak defense against his imagination is the hope that if destiny ("chance") will have him to be king, then destiny will do the dirty work, and he won't have to lift a finger. Chance may crown him without his stirring in his own service. But notice the subjunctive mood of "may": chance *may* take care of the business, but then again, Macbeth may still have to do it himself.

Chaos Is Come Again

OTHELLO: Excellent wretch! Perdition catch my soul
But I do love thee! and when I love thee not,
Chaos is come again.
IAGO: My noble lord—
OTHELLO: What dost thou say, Iago?
IAGO: Did Michael Cassio, when you woo'd my lady,
Know of your love?

OTHELLO Act 3, scene 3, 90–95

By "Excellent wretch" Othello means his new wife, Desdemona, who has just left the scene. Though "wretch" is elsewhere in Shakespeare a term of endearment, it is nonetheless ominous, just like Othello's other oaths in his speech. "Perdition catch my soul but I do love thee" isn't exactly a comforting sentiment; roughly translated, Othello says, "I'll be damned if I don't love you." Thoughts of perdition and chaos aren't the normal signs of a healthy relationship. Othello can only imagine falling out of love with Desdemona as the collapse of all form and order. In effect, his wife is shouldered with the responsibility for Othello's sanity.

So when in this same scene, through Iago's machinations, Othello does fall out of love with Desdemona, he cries "Othello's occupation's gone!" and embarks on a desperate campaign to prove his wife's treachery, a campaign which culminates in his murdering her. Iago hasn't missed a beat; immediately after Othello pronounces his theory of chaos, Iago begins working on the impassioned Moor. He starts by raising doubts about the kind of relationship Othello's friend Cassio has with Desdemona, doubts which explode, within a few hundred lines, into Othello's certainty that he's been cuckolded.

The Course of True Love
Never Did Run Smooth

LYSANDER: Ay me! for aught that I could ever read,
Could ever hear by tale or history,
The course of true love never did run smooth;
But either it was different in blood—
HERMIA: O cross! too high to be enthrall'd to low.
LYSANDER: Or else misgraffèd in respect of years—
HERMIA: O spite! too old to be engag'd to young.
LYSANDER: Or else it stood upon the choice of friends—
HERMIA: O hell! to choose love by another's eyes.

A MIDSUMMER NIGHT'S DREAM   Act 1, scene 1, 132–140

The young lovers Lysander and Hermia, like young lovers in every comedy, have run into trouble at the very start of the

play. Hermia's father has decided that she shall marry Demetrius, not Lysander; if she refuses, she'll have to face the law of
Athens—that is, either death or consignment to a nunnery.
Lysander offers "comfort" with the observation that "the
course of true love never did run smooth," apparently comparing romance to a river current. His examples—which elicit
parallel replies from Hermia—include affairs complicated by
differences in class ("blood") or age, or dictated by relations
("friends"). I haven't quoted the rest of his complaint, expect-
ing that this sample should be enough. (For the rest of the
catalogue, see SWIFT AS A SHADOW.) Hermia's "misgraffèd," by
the way, means "poorly grafted"; she compares marital union
to hybridization. Horticultural metaphors are common in
Shakespeare [see GET THEE TO A NUNNERY].

The Crack of Doom

[A show of eight Kings, the eighth with a glass in his hand, and Banquo last]
MACBETH: Thou art too like the spirit of Banquo; down!
　　　　 Thy crown does sear mine eyeballs. And thy hair,
　　　　 Thou other gold-bound brow, is like the first.
　　　　 A third is like the former. Filthy hags,
　　　　 Why do you show me this?—A fourth? Start, eyes!
　　　　 What, will the line stretch out to th' crack of doom?
　　　　　　　　　　　　　　 MACBETH　Act 4, scene 1, 112–117

In Shakespeare's time, "doom" still had the primary sense
"judgment"; and here he uses it as shorthand for "doomsday"
or Judgment Day, not as a metaphor for personal failure. The
"crack" itself could be one of many things: the peal of an

archangel's trumpet; one of Jehovah's thunderbolts, calling all souls to order; or even the verge of the abyss separating the temporal world from the final kingdom. This last meaning would rely on a relatively new sense of "crack"—as "break" or "fissure," a sense developed only in the sixteenth century. In any case, the "crack of doom" is, as far as Macbeth is concerned, a long ways off.

When, way back in Act 1, three witches prophesied that Macbeth would be king, they also told his friend Banquo that he would beget a dynasty. This prediction has haunted Macbeth, who has indeed become king in accordance with the prophecy; he thinks the crown worthless if he cannot establish a dynasty. After having Banquo murdered, and unsuccessfully attempting to have Banquo's son murdered, Macbeth revisits the witches. When he asks if Banquo's issue will ever really reign in Scotland, Macbeth is shown a pageant of eight kings. These kings represent the Stuart line, legendarily descended from Banquo. At the time of *Macbeth*'s writing, a Stuart— James VI of Scotland—had recently ascended the throne of England as James I. Macbeth's despair over the number of kings —and their family resemblance to Banquo—is therefore flattery of James, whose line, Shakespeare suggests, will rule Scotland *and* England forever.

Cruel to Be Kind

HAMLET: I do repent; but heaven hath pleas'd it so
To punish me with this, and this with me,
That I must be their scourge and minister.
I will bestow him, and will answer well

> The death I gave him. So again good night.
> I must be cruel only to be kind.
> This bad begins and worse remains behind.

HAMLET   Act 3, scene 4, 173–179

In these lines addressed to his mother, Hamlet speaks of two different cruelties. In the first five lines, the prince refers to his own impulsive killing of the courtier Polonius earlier in the scene. Polonius had been snooping on Hamlet's meeting with his mother; and when Hamlet noticed someone stirring behind an arras (wall-hanging), he ran him through—and so ended Polonius's career. Hamlet rationalizes his deed—about 150 lines after the event—by getting the heavens involved: he's "their scourge and minister," he claims, chosen to visit justice on the corrupt. Polonius deserved what he got, but nonetheless Hamlet repents, and prepares to suffer the consequences: Polonius was punished by Hamlet, and Hamlet will be punished for killing Polonius.

But when Hamlet says he "must be cruel only to be kind," he's shifting his attention back to his mother. He has spent the better part of the scene upbraiding her for indulging her new husband, King Claudius, whom Hamlet compares to a "mildewèd ear" [see FLAMING YOUTH]. He must be cruel to his mother, he explains, only to be kind to her—to save her from lapsing any further into sensuality and betrayal of her dead husband. The sentiment—harsh medicine may effect the best cure—is ancient, but Hamlet apparently coins "cruel to be kind," a very common phrase nowadays.

Cudgel Thy Brains

SECOND CLOWN: Who builds stronger than a mason, a shipwright, or a carpenter?

FIRST CLOWN: Ay, tell me that, and unyoke.

SECOND CLOWN: Marry, now I can tell.

FIRST CLOWN: To't.

SECOND CLOWN: Mass, I cannot tell.

FIRST CLOWN: Cudgel thy brains no more about it, for your dull ass will not mend his pace with beating, and when you are ask'd this question next, say "a gravemaker": the houses he makes lasts till doomsday.

HAMLET Act 5, scene 1, 50–59

As they prepare a grave for Hamlet's erstwhile girlfriend Ophelia, two "clowns"—that is, rustic fellows—lighten their work with riddles. The riddle quoted here needs no explanation; what's interesting is the first clown's humorous put-down of his perplexed assistant. As it happens, Shakespeare was the first to use "cudgel" as a verb (the noun had been around, in its archaic forms, since at least the ninth century). In the earlier play *Henry the Fourth, Part 1*, Mistress Quickly reports to Prince Hal that Falstaff had "call'd you Jack, and said he would cudgel you" (Act 3, scene 3). As companion to this literal use—meaning, of course, to beat with a club—Shakespeare introduces here the first figurative use of the verb. The first clown likens the second clown's brain to a dull ass, a sluggish beast of burden, which cannot move any faster ("mend its pace") even if it's clubbed.

Dancing Days

CAPULET: A hall, a hall, give room! And foot it, girls!
        More light, you knaves, and turn the tables up;
        And quench the fire, the room is grown too hot.
        Ah, sirrah, this unlook'd-for sport comes well.
        Nay, sit, nay, sit, good cousin Capulet,
        For you and I are past our dancing days.
        How long is't now since last yourself and I
        Were in a mask?

ROMEO AND JULIET   Act 1, scene 5, 26–33

Old Capulet is throwing a ball. Here he pulls a contemporary off the floor, protesting that "you and I are past our dancing days." His meaning is clear: "Let's not make spectacles of ourselves; we're too old for such strenuous, exhibitionistic activities." Capulet may be referring to a proverb, because the formulation shows up several times within a decade of the first performance of *Romeo and Juliet*. On the other hand, later writers may intend their audiences to recognize the reference to Shakespeare.

At the urging of friends, Romeo crashes Capulet's little party; a little swim with some other fish might help him forget his disdainful lover Rosaline. Romeo comes masked, both to observe custom and to protect himself—his family are sworn enemies of the Capulets. In the prime of his dancing days, the young lover dances indeed—with Juliet, Capulet's daughter.

A Dish Fit for the Gods

BRUTUS: Let's be sacrificers, but not butchers, Caius.
         . . . And, gentle friends,
Let's kill him boldly, but not wrathfully;
Let's carve him as a dish fit for the gods,
Not hew him as a carcass fit for hounds;
And let our hearts, as subtle masters do,
Stir up their servants to an act of rage,
And after seem to chide 'em.

JULIUS CAESAR   Act 2, scene 1, 166, 171–177

Like "sweets to the sweet," this phrase has been wrenched well out of its morbid and somewhat sickening context. To us, a "dish fit for the gods" is delectable or sumptuous. Brutus notes the excellence of the dish, but pursues the gruesome consequences of the metaphor: the dish will have to be cooked—and Julius Caesar is the only ingredient.

Having decided that Caesar's ambitions necessitate his assassination [*see* THE SERPENT'S EGG], Brutus nonetheless cautions his co-conspirators—especially Caius Cassius—against a bloodbath. To hack down Marc Antony as well as Caesar will make the assassins look like "butchers." They ought rather, says Brutus, present themselves as "sacrificers," reluctantly but devoutly offering up Caesar in order to save the Roman Republic. The assassins must appear hesitant (though not unable) to "stir up" the necessary passions (the "servants" of the heart), afterward "chiding" those passions with seeming regret. Unfortunately for Brutus and Cassius, sparing Antony leaves alive the one man whose sense of public relations is even more sophisticated than Brutus's.

"A dish fit for the gods" vaguely recalls the legend of Tantalus, who offered up to the gods an unusual meal—his son Pelops. The gods, however, were not exactly pleased; Tantalus was condemned to suffer eternal hunger and thirst, and his house was cursed. Brutus neglects to pursue the lesson of this famous tale—the stuff of contemporary Roman tragedy—and does so at his peril.

The Dogs of War

MARCUS ANTONIUS: And Caesar's spirit, raging for revenge,
With Ate by his side come hot from hell,
Shall in these confines with a monarch's voice
Cry "Havoc!" and let slip the dogs of war,
That this foul deed shall smell above the earth
With carrion men, groaning for burial.

JULIUS CAESAR Act 3, scene 1, 270–275

Since Julius Caesar's assassination, his right-hand man Marc Antony has had to resort to veiled ironies in putting his own case to the public [see FRIENDS, ROMANS, COUNTRYMEN, LEND ME YOUR EARS]. Privately, he rages. As he prepares to strike back at the assassins, Antony invokes Caesar's spirit and Ate, goddess of ruin and strife. Hot from hell—the pagan catch-all for both the blessed and the damned—Caesar and Ate will charge in with dogs of war, visiting havoc on the conspirators. (The dogs in a sense personify—or "caninify"—war.) At least, these are Antony's superheated imaginings; the final destruction of Brutus and Cassius will have more to do with their bad consciences and tactical errors.

"Cry 'Havoc,' " which also surfaces in *King John*, is derived from the Old French "crier havot"—to send out the signal to begin pillaging. Latter-day usage of "cry havoc" follows Shakespeare in the figurative sense of "call down destruction."

Double, Double Toil and Trouble

WITCHES: Double, double toil and trouble
Fire burn, and cauldron bubble.

MACBETH Act 4, scene 1, 10–11, etc.

Three Scottish witches are going about their business—tossing poisoned entrails, eye of newt, toe of frog, and such, into a cauldron—while awaiting a visit from the man they said would be king: Macbeth. "Double, double toil and trouble" is part of the refrain to their demonic incantation, an inspiring little number in tetrameter (four accents per line). The collective memory has clouded somewhat; often, this refrain comes to mind in the jumbled form "Bubble, bubble, toil and trouble," which makes even less sense than the original. The witches are actually trying, with their spells, to pile up toil and trouble until they "double"—yielding twice the toil and double the trouble for Macbeth, presumably.

He Hath Eaten Me out of House and Home

HOSTESS QUICKLY: He hath eaten me out of house and home, he hath put all my substance into that fat belly of his: but I will have some of it out again, or I will ride thee a-nights like the mare.

FALSTAFF: I think I am as like to ride the mare if I have any vantage of ground to get up.

HENRY THE FOURTH, PART 2   Act 2, scene 1, 74–79

Hostess Quickly of the Boar's-Head Tavern is complaining about her lodger, Sir John Falstaff. The gargantuan knight has been imposing himself and his appetite on the simple woman and has been unforthcoming when faced with the tab. Quickly threatens to visit him like a nightmare; Falstaff retorts with a characteristically obscene reading of her threat.

This famous phrase was first formulated as "He hath eaten me out of house" sometime in the fifteenth century. If one liked, he might also have eaten you "out of house and harbor" or "out of doors," but the Bard seems to have originated the current phrase. The formula "out of house and home" itself dates from about the thirteenth century. It's never been clear whether "home" is being distinguished from "house" or whether the phrase is just a piece of poetry. As we have adopted Quickly's phrasing, however, we mean something like "He has consumed not only my provisions, but furthermore my domestic comfort."

Every Inch a King

GLOUCESTER: The trick of that voice I do well remember;
        Is't not the King?
LEAR: Ay, every inch a king!

KING LEAR   Act 4, scene 6, 106–107

"Every inch a king" is ironically taken at face value nowadays, without the bitter incongruity of the original context. As the blinded and spurned Duke of Gloucester encounters the ragged and spurned King Lear, the two men stage a pathetic reunion. [*See* MORE SINNED AGAINST THAN SINNING and AS FLIES TO

WANTON BOYS ARE WE TO THE GODS.] Gloucester, able to recognize Lear only by his voice, cannot see that Lear has crowned
himself with weeds. Lear, insane, has regressed into delusions
of omnipotence. When Lear madly declares himself "every
inch a king," he states what may be factually accurate, but
what is in dramatic terms a lie. We have watched the king
slowly degenerate after being stripped of power and dignity by
his wicked daughters, and we have heard Lear himself deni-
grate the pomp of kingship.

The Expense of Spirit in a Waste of Shame

Th' expense of spirit in a waste of shame
Is lust in action, and till action, lust
Is perjur'd, murd'rous, bloody, full of blame,
Savage, extreme, rude, cruel, not to trust,
Enjoy'd no sooner but despisèd straight,
Past reason hunted, and no sooner had,
Past reason hated as a swallowed bait
On purpose laid to make the taker mad. . . .

"Sonnet 129," 1–8

The speaker of this sonnet anatomizes lust into its "before" and
"after" states, and concludes that it's a "heaven that leads men
to hell" (line 14). "Lust in action"—that is, lust as it is realized
in actions—is characterized as the expenditure ("expense") of
precious energy ("spirit") on shameful desolation ("a waste of
shame"). The passage from overheated pursuit to empty loath-
ing is a kind of energy drain. Specialists on Shakespeare's
naughty puns point out that "spirit" could also connote sem-

inal fluid—thought, by the way, to be discharged by both men and women. Here, however, the speaker seems concerned only with the male point of view.

Fair Play

BASTARD: O inglorious league!
Shall we, upon the footing of our land,
Send fair-play orders and make compremise,
Insinuation, parley, and base truce
To arms invasive?

KING JOHN Act 5, scene 1, 65–69

BASTARD: According to the fair play of the world,
Let me have audience.

KING JOHN Act 5, scene 2, 118–119

Philip Faulconbridge, the illegitimate son of Richard the Lion-Hearted, is this play's patriotic spokesman. Although, unlike King John, he is a consistent defender of English sovereignty, he is a little inconsistent in his use of the phrase "fair play," which he coins. ("Foul play" had been around since the fifteenth century.) In the first instance, he uses the phrase sarcastically, to denote cowardly courtesy toward the very powers —the Vatican and the French—who are brokering England's future. Having capitulated to the Pope, King John receives in return a pledge to pacify the invading French forces, a "league" Faulconbridge characterizes as "inglorious." He rejects "fair-play orders" and "compremise" (compromise); "fair play" is merely capitulation.

In the second instance, however, Faulconbridge stands upon "fair play," seeking audience with the Pope's legate as courtesy and chivalry demand. Even here, though, there is some sarcasm in the bastard, because his mission is to reject the pact with the Pope and the capitulation to France. "Fair play" is merely customary courtesy, a show of civility to those one detests to the point of bloodshed. What has become for us a mark of civility—playing by the rules of the game—is still for Faulconbridge an ambivalent quality, a not always necessary evil.

A Feast of Languages

ARMADO: *[To Moth]* Chirrah!

HOLOFERNES: *Quare* chirrah, not sirrah?

ARMADO: Men of peace, well encount'red.

HOLOFERNES: Most military sir, salutation.

MOTH: *[Aside to Costard]* They have been at a great feast of languages, and stol'n the scraps.

COSTARD: O, they have liv'd long on the alms-basket of words.

LOVE'S LABOR'S LOST   Act 5, scene 1, 32–39

The schoolmaster Holofernes and the braggart soldier Don Armado engage in their favorite affectation: perversion of speech and indulgence in "ink-horn terms"—studied archaisms and foreign importations. Holofernes' mixing of Latin (*"Quare,"* which means "why") and English is typical, as is Armado's affected "Men of peace," his euphemism for "civilians." Moth (Armado's page) and Costard (a country clown) deliver their common-man's diagnosis of this linguistic disease: the pedant and the braggart have, like poor beggars, stolen the leftovers from some big "feast of languages." Their mottled patchwork of dialects is like an indiscriminate hodgepodge of discards from discrete courses. An "alms-basket" is a basket used to collect charitable donations for the poor; Armado and Holofernes have long dipped into it for their hand-me-down discourse.

Flaming Youth

HAMLET: O shame, where is thy blush?
         Rebellious hell,
         If thou canst mutine in a matron's bones,
         To flaming youth let virtue be as wax
         And melt in her own fire.

                                        HAMLET Act 3, scene 4, 81–85

In the infamous "closet scene," Hamlet delivers a furious lecture to his appalled mother, Queen Gertrude. The prince finally vents his barely repressed resentment of her marriage to her brother-in-law, whom Hamlet considers a very low specimen of slime. After holding up two portraits—one of his murdered father, the other of his despised stepfather—and comparing the latter to a "mildewèd ear" (line 64), Hamlet demands to know how Gertrude could sink so low. Such gross lack of judgment hardly befits an aging matron. According to Hamlet's curious biology, lust ("Rebellious hell") is an infection of the bones, and Gertrude's bones ought to be made of sterner stuff. If the cool constitution of a matron is so vulnerable to lust, then virtue is weak, soft, pliable as wax, and will melt instantly in the flames of youthful passion.

As Flies to Wanton Boys Are We to the Gods

GLOUCESTER: I' th' last night's storm I such a fellow saw,
Which made me think a man a worm. My son
Came then into my mind, and yet my mind
Was then scarce friends with him. I have heard more
        since.
As flies to wanton boys are we to th' gods,
They kill us for their sport.

KING LEAR Act 4, scene 1, 32–37

Perhaps the most desperate lines in a desperate play, the Duke of Gloucester's speech culminates scene after scene of abject cruelty and senseless brutality. For the kindness he has shown the disgraced King Lear on a stormy night [see MORE SINNED AGAINST THAN SINNING], Gloucester has been blinded by two of the king's enemies, Lear's daughter Regan and her husband.

Gloucester, like Lear, has had to face up to cruel revelations. The son he thought treacherous—Edgar—has proved innocent, but only after Gloucester drove him out. He is the worm-like "fellow" Gloucester saw before his blinding—Edgar in disguise as a mad beggar. And like Lear, the pompous Gloucester has been forced to feel what the wretched of the earth feel

—the cruelties of heaven and of mankind alike [*see* TAKE PHYSIC, POMP]. The duke sums up his revelation in two of the most memorable lines in Shakespeare, likening the gods to immature, uncaring, unjust children, and man to insignificant flies, creatures subject to sportful cruelty.

For Goodness' Sake

PROLOGUE: Therefore, for goodness sake, and as you are known
The first and happiest hearers of the town,
Be sad, as we would make ye.

HENRY THE EIGHTH Prologue, 23–25

WOLSEY: For goodness sake, consider what you do,
How you may hurt yourself—ay, utterly
Grow from the King's acquaintance, by this carriage.

HENRY THE EIGHTH Act 3, scene 1, 159–161

It's unusual that the first time a phrase appears in surviving literature it appears twice in the same place. The repetition suggests that the author was used to the phrase, which was perhaps becoming common when *Henry the Eighth* was composed—around 1613. Since the play is apparently a collaboration between Shakespeare and his successor John Fletcher, it's hard to be certain whose words "for goodness sake" are—the prologue, in any case, doesn't sound Shakespearean.

"For goodness' sake"—an Elizabethan wouldn't use the apostrophe as we're required to—has its literal force here: "for the sake of goodness and decency." The prologue petitions the play's first "hearers" (audience) to be "sad" (serious) for the sake of one kind of goodness—politeness or kindness. Cardinal Wolsey—a real snake in the grass—urges Queen Katherine to mend her petulant "carriage" (behavior) for the sake of a more general goodness—goodness in the abstract. As the phrase became more and more common, it lost its status as an adverb and became a simple interjection—just like its counterpart, "For God's sake." We usually use it to verbally throw up our hands rather than to urge any particular action for the sake of goodness.

Foregone Conclusion

OTHELLO: O monstrous, monstrous!
IAGO: Nay, this was but his dream.
OTHELLO: But this denoted a foregone conclusion.
IAGO: 'Tis a shrewd doubt, though it be but a dream,
          And this may help to thicken other proofs,
          That do demonstrate thinly.

OTHELLO Act 3, scene 3, 427–431

Othello—the brave, romantic, and somewhat credulous Moor of Venice—has fallen under the evil spell of his ensign Iago.

Here, Iago pretends that a certain Lieutenant Cassio has been dreaming—audibly—of Othello's chaste wife Desdemona. Othello believes that Cassio's alleged dreams must reenact the "foregone conclusion" of adultery. In Othello's mind, this speculation quickly "thickens" into proof that Desdemona has betrayed him.

When he coins this phrase, Othello seems to mean an adulterous act ("conclusion") which has preceded the dream, or what one editor calls a "previous consummation." But the matter isn't settled, no less in the original than in modern-day speech; "foregone conclusion" becomes only more confusing the more you think about it.

Today we use it to mean "predetermined outcome"—something anybody could have anticipated; but how we got from *Othello* to here is a mystery. Just as we now judge a person's dreams more as a wish for the future than a replay of the past, "conclusion" has come to refer to an inference of what will happen rather than an act that has already occurred.

Fortune's Fool

BENVOLIO: Romeo, away, be gone!
　　　　　The citizens are up, and Tybalt slain.
　　　　　Stand not amaz'd, the Prince will doom thee death
　　　　　If thou art taken. Hence be gone, away!
ROMEO:　　O, I am fortune's fool!

ROMEO AND JULIET　Act 3, scene 1, 132–136

LEAR:　　　　　　　　I am even
　　　The natural fool of fortune.

KING LEAR　Act 4, scene 6, 190–191

TIMON: You fools of fortune. . . .

TIMON OF ATHENS **Act 3, scene 6, 96**

Foolishness fascinated the Bard and his audience; the number of contemporary proverbs about fools is stunning. "A fool's bolt [arrow] is soon shot"; "No fool to [like] the old fool"; "Either a fool or a physician"; "A fool and his money be soon at debate"; "The fool doth think he is wise, but the wise man knows himself to be a fool" (that one's inherited from Socrates); "The first chapter of fools is to hold themselves wise"; "As the fool thinks, so the bell clinks"; "A fool's paradise"; "Fat as a fool"; "Two fools in one house are too many"—just to mention a few.

Shakespeare's phrase "fortune's fool" seems to be his invention, although it has proverbial kin: "Fortune favors fools"; "God sends fortune to fools"; and "Fools have fortune," all of which date from the mid-sixteenth century. In Shakespeare's hands, however, the sentiment of all these proverbs is inverted. Fortune is not bestowed on fools; men are the slaves Fortune makes fools of. Romeo, for example, simply by defending himself against Tybalt, a Capulet and therefore a blood enemy, becomes an outlaw. Caught up in a design he is powerless to affect, Romeo feels like fortune's puppet.

Frailty, Thy Name Is Woman

HAMLET: Heaven and earth,
        Must I remember? Why, she would hang on him
        As if increase of appetite had grown
        By what it fed on, and yet, within a month—
        Let me not think on't—Frailty, thy name is woman!—

HAMLET **Act 1, scene 2, 142–146**

Hamlet, in his first soliloquy, recalls tender scenes between his mother, Queen Gertrude, and her deceased husband. What irks Hamlet is that, after his mother had seemed so sexually dependent on the old king, she could turn around within a month of his death and marry her brother-in-law Claudius, who, Hamlet claims, is "no more like my father/ Than I to Hercules" (lines 152–153) and compares to his father as "Hyperion to a satyr" (line 140)—as the sun-god to a deformed goat-man.

To Hamlet, his mother is the archetypal woman. Her incestuous inconstancy moves him to exclaim, "Frailty, thy name is woman!" It's not so much that Hamlet is a misogynist as that his mother's sexuality has poisoned his own, as we shall see in his relations to Ophelia [*see* GET THEE TO A NUNNERY].

Friends, Romans, Countrymen, Lend Me Your Ears

MARCUS ANTONIUS: Friends, Romans, countrymen, lend me your ears!
      I come to bury Caesar, not to praise him.
      The evil that men do lives after them,
      The good is oft interred with their bones;
      So let it be with Caesar.

JULIUS CAESAR Act 3, scene 2, 74–77

Outside of *Hamlet*, these are likely the most quoted of all Shakespeare's lines. Almost never quoted, however, are the lines Antony is parodying—the opening words of Brutus's earlier oration: "Romans, countrymen, and lovers, hear me for my cause, and be silent that you may hear" (lines 13–14).

Antony later disingenuously claims that "I am no orator, as

Brutus is" (line 217). Yet his modifications of Brutus's formulaic oratory are the first hint that he knows his business. Just compare the deft escalation of rhythm in "Friends, Romans, countrymen" with the metric jangle of "Romans, countrymen, and lovers"; note the arrogance of "be silent" versus the mock humility of "lend me your ears." The contrast is more than literary; Brutus, one of Caesar's assassins, insists he took part in the conspiracy in order to preserve Roman liberties, yet Antony's rhetoric seems much more democratic. Antony skillfully manipulates the crowd where Brutus lectured to it.

Full Circle

EDGAR: The gods are just, and of our pleasant vices
        Make instruments to plague us:
        The dark and vicious place where thee he got
        Cost him his eyes.
EDMUND: Th' hast spoken right, 'tis true.
        The wheel is come full circle, I am here.

                                KING LEAR   Act 5, scene 3, 171–175

"Full circle" is Edmund's coinage, and he employs a now-rare meaning of "full": "complete." The wheel of fortune has completed its circuit, and Edmund's own villainous acts have returned to haunt him. In essence, Edmund's use of "full circle" is close to ours—we too mean that someone's actions have passed through phases only to return to their starting point; but we no longer ascribe the outcome to the inevitable workings of Fate.

Edmund is the bastard son of Edgar's father, the late Duke of Gloucester. The duke has been blinded by Lear's enemies, but Edgar blames this on Gloucester himself. His adulterous lust—the "pleasant vices" that resulted in Edmund's conception—"cost him his eyes." This highly moralistic view of events relies on a notion of divine justice hardly operative in this play. Nonetheless, Edmund must agree; he has just been mortally wounded by his half-brother, and he interprets this as the result of his betrayal of Edgar. The villain Edmund had turned the duke against his legitimate son Edgar; the duke's lust produced Edmund, and therefore Edmund's villainy; Edmund's villainy, now come full circle, produces Edgar's successful revenge.

Get Thee to a Nunnery

HAMLET: I did love you once.
OPHELIA: Indeed, my lord, you made me believe so.
HAMLET: You should not have believ'd me, for virtue cannot so
  inoculate our old stock but we shall relish of it. I lov'd you not.
OPHELIA: I was the more deceiv'd.
HAMLET: Get thee to a nunn'ry, why woulds't thou be a breeder of
  sinners?

HAMLET Act 3, scene 1, 114–121

In this heartbreaking scene, it's hard to tell how much of what Hamlet says is sincere, and how much an act [see ANTIC DISPOSITION]. The critics have never ceased arguing this question. We do know that his mother's recent remarriage has intensified Hamlet's sexual revulsion—he's recently likened the sexual act to tumbling in a sty.

Here, the prince denies ever having loved Ophelia, right after claiming that he did love her once. This may be just a game Hamlet is playing, but perhaps he means that what seemed like love to him once now seems false and repulsive. Using a horticultural metaphor, he casts doubt on his own motives: the "old stock" (original nature) of man is so corrupt that the grafting of virtue can never wholly eradicate the "relish" (taste) of corruption. In his famous line "Get thee to a nunn'ry," he exhorts Ophelia to put herself away so that she may never breed sinners like Hamlet.

Specialists in Shakespeare's bawdy language are fond of noting that "nunnery" was common Elizabethan slang for "brothel," and that therefore Hamlet's command is ironic and even more despairing than it seems. The pun would accord with the paradoxical nature of the prince's speech, but there is little evidence elsewhere in the scene that Hamlet intends a double entendre.

Gilded Monuments

> Not marble nor the gilded monuments
> Of princes shall outlive this pow'rful rhyme,
> But you shall shine more bright in these contents
> Than unswept stone, besmear'd with sluttish time.
>
> "Sonnet 55," 1–4

Optimism isn't the most prominent feature of Shakespeare's sonnets, but here the poet sees a great future for his poem. Addressing himself probably to a young aristocrat, the speaker boasts that while concrete monuments may decay or burn, his poem will escape such ravages of "sluttish time." This sort of brag was the stuff of contemporary defenses of poetry. The memory of an Achilles or an Aeneas would be utterly lost, defenders claimed, if we had to count on "gilded monuments," which are impressive to the eye but helpless before time. The speaker claims to do for his young man what Homer did for Achilles.

Shakespeare's own eulogists reaffirm his perhaps hubristic forecast. Ben Jonson, in the first edition of Shakespeare's collected works, called the Bard a "Moniment [monument], without a tomb," still alive "while thy Book doth live." Later, John Milton wrote Shakespeare an epitaph mocking the notion that the poet would ever require an elaborate structure to house his "honor'd bones." Shakespeare built himself "a lasting Monument," the folio collection of his works, and that is the only "tomb" he will ever need.

The Glass of Fashion

OPHELIA: O, what a noble mind is here o'erthrown!
The courtier's, soldier's, scholar's, eye, tongue, sword,
Th' expectation and rose of the fair state,
The glass of fashion and the mould of form,
Th' observ'd of all observers, quite, quite down!

HAMLET, Act 3, scene 1, 150–154

After Hamlet repeatedly advises her to "get thee to a nunn'ry" [*see* p. 46], Ophelia bewails the noble prince's apparent madness and mourns Denmark's loss of so exemplary a gentleman. Like the society of Shakespeare's England, the society of Hamlet's Denmark seems to operate on a principle of emulation: all noblemen are expected to remark and imitate the manners of the prince. Hamlet's eye (perception), tongue (discourse), and sword (prowess) set standards for courtiers, soldiers, and scholars, if not in that order. Till he went bonkers, he was the chiefest bloom of the realm, the princely paragon observed by all observers. Hamlet was the "glass of fashion": that is, the mirror of comportment. "Glass" commonly meant "mirror" in Shakespeare's day; "fashion" was more ambiguous, meaning fashion as we know it, but more commonly what Ophelia also calls "form": "manner," "demeanor," or "self-disposition."

Good Riddance

AJAX: I shall cut out your tongue.
THERSITES: 'Tis no matter, I shall speak as much as thou afterwards.
PATROCLUS: No more words, Thersites, peace!
THERSITES: I will hold my peace when Achilles' brach bids me, shall I?
ACHILLES: There's for you, Patroclus.
THERSITES: I will see you hang'd like clatpoles ere I come any more to your tents. I will keep where there is wit stirring, and leave the faction of fools. [*Exit*]
PATROCLUS: A good riddance.

TROILUS AND CRESSIDA   Act 2, scene 1, 110–120

The *Oxford English Dictionary* lists no use of "(a) good riddance" before 1782, although it does cite Portia's "a gentle riddance" from the earlier *Merchant of Venice* (Act 2, scene 7) in its entry for "riddance." Portia means the same thing Patroclus means: "glad to be rid of you." We have preserved the phrase only in the form "good riddance," dropping the article "a"—the phrase is less descriptive now, and more expletive. We don't really think of "riddance" as a noun, which might be modified by adjectives such as "good," "gentle," "fair," or "bad."

In this case, Patroclus, a Greek warrior dear to Achilles, expresses relief as the satirical rogue Thersites departs. Thersites makes a sport of mocking fellow Greeks who have pretensions to valor, honor, and such like qualities. Here he deflates Patroclus by calling him "Achilles' brach"—that is, "Achilles' bitch"—an indecent characterization of the intimate friendship between Achilles and Patroclus. Spurned, Thersites vows to see this crowd "hang'd like clatpoles" before he comes back to their tents to "entertain" them again. In Elizabethan slang, "clatpole" or "clotpole" meant "blockhead" or "wooden head," which Thersites imagines being hung from a rope. "Clotpole" derives from "clodpoll."

The Green-Eyed Monster

IAGO: O, beware, my lord, of jealousy;
        It is the green-ey'd monster, which doth mock
        The meat it feeds on. That cuckold lives in bliss,
        Who, certain of his fate, loves not his wronger:
        But O, what damnèd minutes tells he o'er
        Who dotes, yet doubts, suspects, yet strongly loves!

OTHELLO: O misery!

OTHELLO **Act 3, scene 3, 165–171**

The notion that jealousy is green-eyed is probably older than Shakespeare, although Shakespeare is our earliest authority in print. In *The Merchant of Venice*, Portia refers to "green-eyed jealousy" (Act 3, scene 2), and here Shakespeare coins the more intense phrase "green-ey'd monster." Renaissance Englishmen often paired colors with emotions or personal qualities: both green and yellow are emblematic of jealousy, and green is also emblematic of envy. Some colors are associated with the bodily fluids or "humors" thought to make up the temperament; green and black were the colors attributed to bile.

Iago's basic idea is that the fortunate man *knows* his wife is cheating; the unfortunate man only *suspects* it, and is caught between the jaws of affection and anxiety. History and Shakespeare's infinity of cuckold jokes testify that Renaissance men were particularly prone to suspect their wives. The social perils of cuckoldry were severe indeed: it ruined a man's credit and debased his wife. Such consequences produced an advanced state of jealous suspicion known as "horn-madness," named after the metaphorical horns that were supposed to sprout from the cuckold's brow.

Hath Not a Jew Eyes?

SHYLOCK: I am a Jew. Hath not a Jew eyes? Hath not a Jew hands, organs, dimensions, senses, affections, passions; fed with the same food, hurt with the same weapons, subject to the same diseases, heal'd by the same means, warm'd and cool'd by the same winter and summer, as a Christian is? If you prick us, do we not bleed? If you tickle us, do we not laugh? If you poison us, do we not die? And if you wrong us, do we not revenge? If we are like you in the rest, we will resemble you in that.

THE MERCHANT OF VENICE   Act 3, scene 1, 58–68

After a Christian has eloped with his daughter, and after the pair have made off with a portion of his ducats, Shylock confronts two other taunting Christians. When they've finished mocking him, they ask whether Shylock seriously intends to take a pound of Antonio's flesh if the merchant defaults on his loan [see POUND OF FLESH]. Shylock affirms that he is indeed serious, especially given his recent indignities at the hands of Christians. "Hath not a Jew eyes?" he asks rhetorically; Jews suffer, bleed, and die just like Christians do, and are just as susceptible to the urge for revenge. The Christians of the play universally assume that they're a nobler species than Jews, but Shylock insists that they're no more pure than Jews and Jews no less human than Christians. There's no little pathos in Shylock's speeches, even though his main purpose in the play is to be villainous. Both Shylock *and* the Christians have lessons to learn, before this play is over, about humaneness and humility.

In My Heart of Hearts

HAMLET: Give me that man
        That is not passion's slave, and I will wear him
        In my heart's core, ay, in my heart of heart,
        As I do thee.

                                    HAMLET   Act 3, scene 2, 71–74

The Bard was a logical man, and he went about coining sensible phrases in a rational fashion. Thus, Hamlet does not say "in my heart of hearts," but "in my heart of heart"—that is, at the "heart" (center) of my heart. The phrase is in fact a synonym for "In my heart's core." And like the heart of an artichoke, the heart of Hamlet's heart is its most tender part. He reserves this region of his affection for men who aren't slaves to their passion, who are governed by reason, like his friend Horatio (whom he addresses here) and, indeed, like the phrase-coining Shakespeare.

We've perverted the phrase into "in my heart of hearts" by way of expressions like Ecclesiastes' "vanity of vanities." But where Ecclesiastes had a number of vanities from which to elect a chief or encompassing vanity—presumption—one doesn't have a number of hearts. Even granting that we use "heart" mostly as a metaphor and not with reference to the organ, we never mean to speak of having more than one.

Heart on My Sleeve

IAGO: It is as sure as you are Roderigo,
Were I the Moor, I would not be Iago.
In following him, I follow but myself;
Heaven is my judge, not I for love and duty,
But seeming so, for my peculiar end;
For when my outward action doth demonstrate
The native act and figure of my heart
In complement extern, 'tis not long after
But I will wear my heart upon my sleeve
For daws to peck at. I am not what I am.

OTHELLO Act 1, scene 1, 56–65

The ever-inventive Iago confesses to his dupe Roderigo that he only *seems* loyal to (only *seems* to "follow") the Venetian general, Othello. Actually, Iago serves only himself and his "peculiar end," or selfish aims. Discretion is required: in Iago's paranoid world, revealing your true motives makes you a victim. To express outwardly in "complement extern" the "native act and figure" of one's heart is to manifest externally the inmost shape and tendency of one's desires. Doing so, Iago says, soon leads to betrayal; when your heart is displayed so openly, as if upon your sleeve, the "daws" (jackdaws) will accept the invitation to peck away at it.

By admitting to his treachery, Iago would seem, in effect, to "wear his heart on his sleeve" for Roderigo. Yet, while Iago tells the truth, he doesn't tell all of it, and keeps hidden his true "native act and figure"—his intention to dupe Roderigo out of even more jewels and cash.

A Hit, a Very Palpable Hit

HAMLET: Come on, sir.
LAERTES: Come, my lord.
     [*They play and Hamlet scores a hit*]
HAMLET: One.
LAERTES: No.
HAMLET: Judgment.
OSRIC: A hit, a very palpable hit.
LAERTES: Well, again.
KING: Stay, give me drink. Hamlet, this pearl is thine,
    Here's to thy health! Give him the cup.

HAMLET   Act 5, scene 2, 280–283

This fencing match between Prince Hamlet and Laertes seems innocent, but will be deadly. King Claudius and Laertes, each for his own reason, have conspired to murder the prince while pretending to sport with him [see THERE'S SPECIAL PROVIDENCE IN THE FALL OF A SPARROW]. The tip of Laertes' foil is poisoned; one successful "hit" will do Hamlet in. Hamlet, however, takes the first point, as judged by the otherwise sycophantic Osric, who saw Hamlet's "very palpable hit." "Palpable," though it had originally meant "sensible to the touch," by the fifteenth century had come to mean "readily perceived by any of the five senses"—in other words, "obvious." In this case, Osric's use of the word is felicitous; when Hamlet is palpably hit, he will definitely feel it.

The king is easily excited. When Laertes loses the first point, Claudius nervously adopts his second strategy: to poison Hamlet with a cup of wine. He ostentatiously plunks a poisoned pearl in the drink he offers to his stepson. Unfortunately for the king, Hamlet refuses the offer, but the queen drinks. And while Hamlet is dying from the poison on Laertes' foil, he forces the rest of the wine down Claudius's throat. A fitting end for a man born to the manner of carousing.

Hob Nob

VIOLA: I pray you sir, what is he?

SIR TOBY: He is knight, dubb'd with unhatch'd rapier, and on carpet consideration, but he is a devil in private brawl. Souls and bodies hath he divorc'd three, and his incensement at this moment is so implacable, that satisfaction can be none but by pangs of death and sepulchre. Hob, nob, is his word; give't or take't.

TWELFTH NIGHT Act 3, scene 4, 234–240

The phrase "hab nab"—or "hab or nab"—had been around for about seventy years when Shakespeare's Sir Toby Belch put an irreversible spin on it and gave us "hob nob." "Hab" probably originated as a verbal form, perhaps as a particular mood of "have"; "hab nab" would then be akin to other verbal phrases such as "willy nilly" ("will I, nill I"). In older English, some verbs could be negated by changing the first letter to "n"; the "nill" of "nill I," for example, means "will not." If this model applies to "hab nab," then "nab" means "hab not" or "have not." As we can see from Sir Toby's phrasing, he equates "hob, nob" with "give't or take't," that is, give the knight the stab or take it from him.

The phrase went through some interesting twists after Shakespeare; "hob, nob" became a drinker's phrase, referring to the trading off of draughts. Almost immediately the phrase was turned into a verb, was eventually cleaned up a little, and came to mean "fraternize" or "hold familiar conversation." In a continuing process of gentrification, the phrase arrived at its present-day meaning.

Hoist with His Own Petard

HAMLET: There's letters seal'd, and my two schoolfellows,
Whom I will trust as I will adders fang'd—
They bear the mandate, they must sweep my way
And marshal me to knavery. Let it work;
For 'tis the sport to have the enginer
Hoist with his own petard, an't shall go hard
But I will delve one yard below their mines
And blow them at the moon.

HAMLET Act 3, scene 4, 202–209

"Hoist with his own petard" literally means "blown up with his own mine." More generally, a "petard" is a hat-shaped device which can be be charged with gunpowder. Here's how Hamlet arrives at the phrase:

The prince—having "caught the conscience" of the murderous King Claudius [*see* THE PLAY'S THE THING]—is about to be packed off on a little vacation to England. He apparently hasn't been feeling too well in the head, so the king orders Hamlet's old school chums Rosencrantz and Guildenstern to keep him company. Though the two fools are relatively innocent (for spies), Hamlet knows that Claudius has some "knavery" planned and that Rosencrantz and Guildenstern are the king's tools.

Hamlet has already guessed that the letters his schoolfellows are carrying to the English court bear a "mandate" for his immediate execution. The prince intends to hoise this mine in the king's face. Claudius is the "enginer," the deviser of the explosive; and his plot is about a yard shallower than that of his nephew, who will send Rosencrantz and Guildenstern to the fate intended for himself.

Hold a Mirror Up to Nature

HAMLET: Suit the action to the word, the word to the action, with this special observance, that you o'erstep not the modesty of nature: for any thing so o'erdone is from the purpose of playing, whose end, both at the first and now, was and is, to hold as 'twere the mirror up to nature: to show virtue her feature, scorn her own image, and the very age and body of the time his form and pressure.

HAMLET Act 3, scene 2, 17–24

Hamlet lectures the actors who will soon perform for his step-father [see TRIPPINGLY ON THE TONGUE]. As director, he expounds the "purpose of playing," which, from the invention of theater, has been to hold "the mirror up to nature." Here, Hamlet echoes classical authors, who insisted that drama be a form of truth, not mere entertainment. Playwrights and players should strive to present action in the most verisimilar manner, without exaggeration or distortion, without bombast or excessive sentimentality. In the theatrical mirror we see our virtues and vices reflected back to us in their true shape: that's the theater's moral function. Defensive dramatists, who had to contend with accusations of corrupting the masses, were fond of pointing out that their productions did indeed have the effect Hamlet advertises [see THE PLAY'S THE THING].

A Horse, a Horse! My Kingdom for a Horse!

KING RICHARD: A horse, a horse! My kingdom for a horse!
CATESBY: Withdraw, my lord; I'll help you to a horse.
KING RICHARD: Slave! I have set my life upon a cast,
     And I will stand the hazard of the die.

RICHARD THE THIRD   Act 5, scene 4, 7–10

Alternately pathetic and arrogant, the hunchbacked villain-king Richard III is about to meet his doom at the hands of the future Henry VII. Richard's most memorable line is actually supposed to sound halfway valiant—he refuses to forsake the fray although his horse has bit the dust. But even in its day, the line became the stuff of irreverent quotation. Shakespeare's contemporary, the playwright, satirist, and cad John Marston, parodied Richard's outcry obsessively ("A boat, a boat, a boat, a full hundred marks for a boat!"; "A fool, a fool, a fool, my coxcomb for a fool!"—a coxcomb is a fool's cap). Marston set the decidedly less than hilarious pace for generations of wits: the line is always good for a cheap laugh.

Household Words

KING HENRY: This day is call'd the feast of Crispian:
           He that outlives this day, and comes safe home,
           Will stand a' tiptoe when this day is named,
           And rouse him at the name of Crispian. . . .
           Old men forget; yet all shall be forgot,
           But he'll remember with advantages
           What feats he did that day. Then shall our names,
           Familiar in his mouth as household words . . .
           Be in their flowing cups freshly rememb'red.
           HENRY THE FIFTH Act 4, scene 3, 40–55

Camped outside Agincourt, where he will successfully consummate his invasion of France, King Henry V rouses the troops in his inimitable style [*see* ONCE MORE UNTO THE BREACH]. Just in case his men were losing faith—the English are vastly outnumbered—Henry appeals to the pride and glory, not of war, but of old men's tales of war. Victory will bring a kind of immortality, because the names of the heroes will become as familiar in English mouths as their "household words." As we do, Henry uses "household" to connote extreme familiarity. At home, people are just people, not specialists of any variety, and they speak the commonest language. Oddly, this elitism-in-reverse is meant to ensure the greatest distinction—familiarity breeds, not contempt, but glory, even immortality. Henry and Shakespeare's audience appreciated this phenomenon as the distinction of the hero; that we now expand it to include consumer products and media celebrities does, perhaps, verge on contempt.

An Improbable Fiction

MARIA: Get him to say his prayers, good Sir Toby, get him to pray.
MALVOLIO: My prayers, minx!
MARIA: No; I warrant you, he will not hear of godliness.
MALVOLIO: Go hang yourselves all! You are idle shallow things, I am not of your element. You shall know more hereafter. [Exit]
SIR TOBY: Is't possible?
FABIAN: If this were play'd upon a stage now, I could condemn it as an improbable fiction.

TWELFTH NIGHT   Act 3, scene 4, 118–128

Irritated by Malvolio's killjoy interference with their reveling, Maria, Sir Toby Belch, and their crew have taken revenge by duping Malvolio into absolutely mad behavior [see LAUGH ONE-SELF INTO STITCHES]. The lady of the house, Olivia, spurns Malvolio's new fashions and his provocative advances as "midsummer madness" and puts him in the care of his enemies, who here continue to torment him. The conspirator Fabian, awed at the improbable ease with which Malvolio swallowed the bait, compares recent events to a bad play. (This isn't the first or last time Shakespeare has a character call attention to his status as part of a fiction, though this is one of the most famous instances.) The reason an "improbable fiction" is to be condemned has mostly to do with the critical dogma of the age, inherited from Aristotle. Probability—the sense that what goes on on stage could actually be taking place in real life—was supposed to be the sine qua non of comic drama. Fabian, Shakespeare, and everyone in the audience, however, know that Malvolio's improbable gullibility makes for satisfying entertainment, Aristotle or no Aristotle.

Her Infinite Variety

MAECENAS: Now Antony
          Must leave her utterly.
ENOBARBUS: Never, he will not:
          Age cannot wither her, nor custom stale
          Her infinite variety. Other women cloy
          The appetites they feed, but she makes hungry
          Where most she satisfies. . . .

ANTONY AND CLEOPATRA   Act 2, scene 2, 232–237

Marc Antony, in a bid to make peace with his fellow triumvir Caesar Augustus, has agreed to marry Caesar's sister. Caesar's friend Maecenas concludes that Antony will now have to give up his infamous affair with Cleopatra, the queen of Egypt, but Enobarbus replies that this is impossible. Unlike other women, he claims, Cleopatra can never grow "stale" with "custom" (familiarity); her charms never fade, they only, in their infinite variety, grow more compelling with time. Enobarbus turns out to be correct; though Antony might sincerely intend to break with Cleopatra, her hold on him overwhelms all considerations of state, and soon he returns to her.

Enobarbus's paean to Cleopatra's erotic power recalls Hamlet's description of how his father enthralled his mother. "Why, she would hang on him," he recalls, "As if increase of appetite had grown/ By what it fed on" (*Hamlet*, Act 1, scene 2). But Hamlet makes no claims to his father's "infinite variety." Variety, allegedly a hallmark of the female nature, was often feared and derided; women's changefulness threatened wooers and husbands alike. In Cleopatra, however, variety becomes a species of excitement, a power to hold on to a lover by keeping love fresh.

Infirm of Purpose

LADY MACBETH: Why did you bring these daggers from the place?
They must lie there. Go carry them, and smear
The sleepy grooms with blood.

MACBETH: I'll go no more.
I am afraid to think what I have done;
Look on't again I dare not.

LADY MACBETH: Infirm of purpose!
Give me the daggers. The sleeping and the dead
Are but as pictures; 'tis the eye of childhood
That fears a painted devil.

MACBETH   Act 2, scene 2, 45–52

As Macbeth returns from murdering King Duncan, Lady Macbeth upbraids him for bringing back incriminating evidence. She thinks that planting the murder weapon on the king's unconsious grooms and smearing them with Duncan's blood will clear her and her husband of any suspicion. This ploy doesn't work, but nevertheless she and Macbeth are not immediately discovered.

When Lady Macbeth calls her husband "infirm of purpose," she refers back to the root meaning of "infirm": unsteady, "not firm." Macbeth's resolve ("purpose") is weak; he fears the deed he's done, and thus he's also "infirm" in the modern sense: his will is crippled. Shakespeare was the first to use the word "infirm" to refer to physical infirmity—in the sense of weakness or disease—but not in *Macbeth*. The heroine of *All's Well that Ends Well* (1601) tells the sickly King of France that she is able to heal him, and that "What is infirm from your sound [healthy] parts shall fly" (Act 2, scene 1, 167).

An Itching Palm

CASSIUS: In such a time as this it is not meet
That every offense should bear his comment.
BRUTUS: Let me tell you, Cassius, you yourself
Are much condemn'd to have an itching palm,
To sell and mart your offices for gold
To undeservers.
CASSIUS: I, an itching palm!

JULIUS CAESAR   Act 4, scene 3, 7–12

"An itching palm" is one that must be scratched with coins. Brutus's dermatological metaphor implies that Cassius's desire for gold—which leads to the sale ("mart") of favors—is unconscious and compulsive. Cassius doesn't think, he just scratches.

Brutus and Cassius, his co-commander, are preparing for battle with Marc Antony and Octavius, who are bent on avenging the murder of Julius Caesar and on securing power in Rome. This is no time, as Cassius says, for comment on every petty offense. But Brutus is too angry—he thinks Cassius deliberately withheld necessary finances from him—to let the matter rest. The two will eventually make amends, after elaborate (and stereotypically Roman) gestures toward suicide.

A King of Infinite Space

HAMLET: To me [Denmark] is a prison.

ROSENCRANTZ: Why then your ambition makes it one. 'Tis too narrow for your mind.

HAMLET: O God, I could be bounded in a nutshell, and count myself a king of infinite space—were it not that I have bad dreams.

GUILDENSTERN: Which dreams indeed are ambition, for the very substance of the ambitious is merely the shadow of a dream.

HAMLET   Act 2, scene 2, 251–259

Denmark isn't a place, it's a state of mind, and Hamlet feels like a prisoner there [*see* THERE'S NOTHING EITHER GOOD OR BAD, BUT THINKING MAKES IT SO]. King Claudius's foolish spies, Rosencrantz and Guildenstern, can't imagine what's wrong with Denmark—it looks like a fine enough place to them. Perhaps, they guess, Hamlet just resents his stepfather's rise to power, which has kept Hamlet from the throne; or perhaps Hamlet thinks Denmark too puny a kingdom to rule anyway.

Hamlet replies that the space inside a nutshell would be a kingdom enough if it were an untroubled kingdom. Kingship is merely an idea, a symbolic form; but the idea has been poisoned by the deeds of the current king and queen of Denmark. Haunted by those deeds as well as by the ghost of his father, Hamlet's world is a bad dream. The dim-witted Guildenstern can only insist glibly on his clichéd notion of a prince's vaulting ambition.

Knock, Knock! Who's There?

PORTER: Here's a knocking indeed! If a man were porter of Hell Gate,
he should have old turning the key. [*Knock*] Knock, knock,
knock! Who's there, i' th' name of Belzebub? . . . [*Knock*] Knock,
knock! Who's there, in th' other devil's name?

MACBETH Act 2, scene 3, 1–8

On August 19, 1936, the entertainment industry trade magazine *Variety* reported that a " 'Knock Knock' craze" was sweeping America. A few months later, on the evening of November
14, a radio performer named Wee Georgie Wood set England
afire with "Knock Knock" jokes. From its disreputable begin-
nings—as a formula for tasteless puns—the "Knock Knock"
joke emerged to take the English-speaking world by storm. In
these days of decline, "Knock, knock! Who's there?" calls
forth yawns more often than giggles, and chiming "Knock,
knock!" is merely a cute substitute for actually knocking on
someone's door.

Although there's no direct line of descent, it's possible that
the birth of "Knock Knock" jokes in the dim recesses of our
century owes more than a little to the famous "porter scene"
in *Macbeth*. The clownish porter tends the gate at Macbeth's
castle, where that notable thane has just successfully murdered
the king of Scotland. In the previous scene, in which Macbeth
and his wife complete the deed, the knocking sounds that
eventually rouse the porter scare the conspiratorial couple out
of their wits: knocking is the sound that crystallizes their guilt.
The porter's joking reference to "Hell Gate" has, then, some
resonance: Macbeth's castle is and will remain the diabolical
duo's headquarters, and the scene of numerous hideous crimes.
The joke also refers obliquely to an earlier dramatic form in
which Hell Gate was an actual prop, and in which the drama

of temptation, sin, salvation, and damnation was materialized to edify the common people. *Macbeth* supplies the tradition with psychological depth.

The Lady Doth Protest too Much

PLAYER QUEEN: Both here and hence pursue me lasting strife,
If once I be a widow, ever I be a wife!
PLAYER KING: 'Tis deeply sworn. Sweet, leave me here a while,
My spirits grow dull, and fain I would beguile
The tedious day with sleep.
PLAYER QUEEN: Sleep rock thy brain,
And never come mischance between us twain!
HAMLET: Madam, how like you this play?
QUEEN: The lady doth protest too much, methinks.

HAMLET Act 3, scene 2, 222–230

Almost always misquoted as "Methinks the lady doth protest too much," Queen Gertrude's line is both drier than the misquotation (thanks to the delayed "methinks") and much more ironic. Prince Hamlet's question is intended to smoke out his mother, to whom, as he intended, this Player Queen bears some striking resemblances [see THE PLAY'S THE THING]. The queen in the play, like Gertrude, seems too deeply attached to her first husband to ever even consider remarrying; Gertrude, however, after the death of Hamlet's father, *has* remarried. We don't know whether Gertrude ever made the same sorts of promises to Hamlet's father that the Player Queen makes to the Player King (who will soon be murdered)—but the irony of her response should be clear.

By "protest," Gertrude doesn't mean "object" or "deny"—

these meanings postdate *Hamlet.* The principal meaning of "protest" in Shakespeare's day was "vow" or "declare solemnly," a meaning preserved in our use of "protestation." When we smugly declare that "the lady doth protest too much," we almost always mean that the lady *objects* so much as to lose credibility. Gertrude says that Player Queen *affirms* so much as to lose credibility. Her vows are too elaborate, too artful, too insistent. More cynically, the queen may also imply that such vows are silly in the first place, and thus may indirectly defend her own remarriage.

Laid on with a Trowel

CELIA: *Bon jour,* Monsieur Le Beau. What's the news?
LE BEAU: Fair princess, you have lost much good sport.
CELIA: Sport! of what color?
LE BEAU: What color, madam? How shall I answer you?
ROSALIND: As wit and fortune will.
TOUCHSTONE: Or as the Destinies decrees.
CELIA: Well said—that was laid on with a trowel.

AS YOU LIKE IT   Act 1, scene 2, 97–106

No doubt, masons and bricklayers, when discussing their mortar, had used the phrase "laid on with a trowel" long before Shakespeare got to it; but its metaphorical and proverbial forms are probably the Bard's invention. The young lady Celia uses the figure to describe language that's plastered on, not with workmanlike care, but with unsubtle force. The clown Touchstone's inflated language itself parodies the lady Rosalind's courtly discourse, just as Rosalind makes fun of Le Beau's unspontaneous phraseology. While Celia refers to Touchstone's crude linguistic workmanship, our use of the phrase is slightly different. Le Beau's sort of "polite" language, a little too elegant and weighty for the situation, is the usual object of the phrase "laid on with a trowel"—eagerly flattering speech.

What Le Beau has come to announce is a wrestling match —the "good sport" sponsored by Celia's uncle, who is now Duke. At this match, Rosalind will meet her future husband, but they won't be married before Shakespeare has put them through the comic wringer.

Laugh Oneself into Stitches

MARIA: If you desire the spleen, and will laugh yourselves into stitches, follow me. Yon gull Malvolio is turn'd heathen, a very renegado; for there is no Christian that means to be sav'd by believing rightly can ever believe such impossible passages of grossness. He's in yellow stockings.

SIR TOBY: And cross-garter'd?

MARIA: Most villainously; like a pedant that keeps a school i' th' church.

TWELFTH NIGHT Act 3, scene 2, 68–76

The noun "stitch" originally meant "a stab," as with a sharp implement. From this meaning we have derived most other senses of the word, as a noun or verb. One "stitches" cloth by stabbing it with a needle; one gets "stitches" from jogging and experiences stabbing pains. Maria, inviting her cohorts to "laugh yourselves into stitches," refers to the facial contortions and stabbing pains induced by the strenuously aerobic activity of laughing. Such hilarity, in Renaissance psychobiology, was thought to reside in the spleen, also the seat of other sudden passions. What will rouse this organ is the sight of the steward

Malvolio who, duped into thinking his employer, the lady Olivia, is in love with him, has also been duped into thinking she has a fetish for yellow stockings and cross-garters. These hideously affected fashions, which are hardly in Malvolio's style, will only help convince Olivia that Malvolio is mad. .

A Lean and Hungry Look

CAESAR:	Antonio!
MARCUS ANTONIUS:	Caesar?
CAESAR:	Let me have men about me that are fat,
	Sleek-headed men and such as sleep a-nights.
	Yond Cassius has a lean and hungry look,
	He thinks too much; such men are dangerous.

JULIUS CAESAR Act 1, scene 2, 190–195

Cassius appears a little underfed these days. His "lean and hungry look" unsettles Julius Caesar, who prefers the company of fat, contented men—who wouldn't bite the hand that feeds them. Cassius looks like he's been up late nursing his envy, a situation that bodes ill for the dictator. Caesar's intuition is accurate: Cassius will spearhead the plot to assassinate him [*see* MASTERS OF THEIR FATES].

Marcus Antonius tries to soothe Caesar: "Fear him not, Caesar, he's not dangerous,/ He is a noble Roman, and well given." Ironically, the superstitious Caesar, who sees through Cassius's noble exterior, will die, while the deluded Antony will survive to avenge him, and later to take power.

Let's Kill All the Lawyers

ALL: God save your majesty!
CADE: I thank you, good people—there shall be no money; all shall eat and drink on my score, and I will apparel them all in one livery, that they may agree like brothers, and worship me their lord.
DICK: The first thing we do, let's kill all the lawyers.
CADE: Nay, that I mean to do.

HENRY THE SIXTH, PART 2 Act 4, scene 2, 71–78

Dick the butcher, a character no one remembers, utters one of the few memorable lines from the entire three-part *Henry the Sixth* cycle. Dick's utopian idea to kill all England's lawyers is his addition to the promises of the traitorous Jack Cade, who envisions a quasi-communistic social revolution, with himself installed as autocrat. Cade alleges that all lawyers do is shuffle parchments back and forth in a systematic attempt to ruin the common people. His demagoguery is simply a calculated appeal to simple folks' longing to be left alone. Yet one may recognize Cade's moral failings and still sympathize with Dick.

In 1987, three Supreme Court Justices convened for a mock

trial, in which representatives of the poetaster Edward de Vere, the 17th Earl of Oxford (1550–1604), challenged Shakespeare's authorship of the plays. The president of American University in Washington, D.C., which sponsored the event, "drew some nervous laughter from the legal contingent in the crowd," the *New York Times* reported, "when he yielded to the temptation to quote the world's most-quoted English author (whoever he was) by saying, 'The first thing we do, let's kill all the lawyers. . . .' " Unsurprisingly, the justices ruled in favor of the Bard of Avon.

Life's Fitful Fever

MACBETH: Better be with the dead
            Whom we, to gain our peace, have sent to peace,
            Than on the torture of the mind to lie
            In restless ecstasy. Duncan is in his grave;
            After life's fitful fever he sleeps well.

MACBETH Act 3, scene 2, 19–23

Lady Macbeth unsuccessfully tries to convince her husband that "what's done, is done" [*see* p. 181]. Macbeth had foreseen that the murder of King Duncan and the seizure of his throne would not be the "be-all and the end-all" [*see* p. 5] of the matter, but that doesn't stave off the inevitable psychological consequences. Beleaguered by bloody hallucinations and guilt-induced fantasies, Macbeth has gotten no peace by satisfying his ambitions. He experiences life, rather, as a "fitful fever," that is, a fever that comes in fits, the heat of ambition alternating with deadly cold, turbulence broken by only transient calms. The dead, he concludes, are truly at peace; murderers and the rest of the living suffer only uncertainty and agitation, as if life were a disease.

Light, Seeking Light, Doth Light of Light Beguile

BEROWNE: Why! all delights are vain, but that most vain
        Which, with pain purchas'd, doth inherit pain:
        As, painfully to pore upon a book
        To seek the light of truth, while truth the while
        Doth falsely blind the eyesight of his look.
        Light, seeking light, doth light of light beguile;
        So ere you find where light in darkness lies,
        Your light grows dark by losing of your eyes.

                                LOVE'S LABOR'S LOST   Act 1, scene 1, 72–79

Berowne's speech has hardly been embraced in everyday English, but it should be better remembered. "Light, seeking light, doth light of light beguile" has all the makings of a proverb. The very absurdity of the alliteration and the self-conscious sophistry of Berowne's "proof" only make the line more charming.

The occasion for Berowne's remarks is a pact drawn up by the King of Navarre, requiring its signatories to forsake for three years the company of women and all other "trivial" pleasures, such as regular meals. The King's object is to establish a "little academe" (he invents the word "academe," by way of Plato); in it, he and his fellows will pursue wisdom with such dedication that their fame will spread across space and time. Berowne's objection, as contrived as it sounds, has an essential grain of wisdom. Staring too long at books, he argues, is painful; why should anyone give up pleasures in order to pursue pain? Reading is blinding: "Light" (the eye), by "seeking light" (in seeking truth), "doth light of light beguile" (deprives itself of vision). If you think you're going to find "truth" in the dark recesses of books, pretty soon you'll be plunged in despair, because blindness will bar you from truth.

What Light through Yonder Window Breaks?

ROMEO: But soft, what light through yonder window breaks?
        It is the east, and Juliet is the sun.
        Arise, fair sun, and kill the envious moon,
        Who is already sick and pale with grief
        That thou, her maid, art far more fair than she.

ROMEO AND JULIET **Act 2, scene 2, 2–6**

In any Shakespeare play written more than a few years after *Romeo and Juliet*, these lines would be laughable; Romeo trots out some of the most clichéd fancies of the day. But the fact that an idea was tired did not necessarily mean it was presented in jest, especially in the years when formulaic sonnets were the rage.

That Juliet is fairer and more brilliant than the moon is meant to be taken as Romeo's sincere belief. When Juliet appears above, on her balcony, she appears like the sun at dawn, her light overpowering the moon's merely reflected brilliance. This is just one in a long series of metaphorical associations of Juliet with light; they begin at the masked ball [see DANCING DAYS], when Romeo exclaims that Juliet "doth teach the torches to burn bright!" (Act 1, scene 5, 44). Later, as Romeo is about to poison himself over what he thinks is Juliet's corpse, he insists twice that all light has been extinguished.

A Long Farewell to All My Greatness

WOLSEY: So farewell—to the little good you bear me.
Farewell? a long farewell to all my greatness!
This is the state of man: to-day he puts forth
The tender leaves of hopes, to-morrow blossoms,
And bears his blushing honors thick upon him;
The third day comes a frost, a killing frost,
And when he thinks, good easy man, full surely
His greatness is a-ripening, nips his root,
And then he falls as I do.

HENRY THE EIGHTH Act 3, scene 2, 350–358

Cardinal Wolsey, the most interesting character in this play, is considerably ambitious. By becoming the chief advisor to the king, he has furthered his plots to amass wealth and secure the

Papacy—the ultimate form he imagines his "greatness" will take. After a series of successes in foiling his enemies, however, Wolsey is exposed. Here, he bitterly calls after his antagonists, who have come to taunt him, and then falls meditatively into a fine soliloquy, one of the few memorable passages in the play.

By "greatness," then, Wolsey means "power." His bitter farewell to political esteem and influence is pretty ironic, considering that he *is* the cardinal. In his current state of mind, he sees the reversal of his fortunes as the workings of a malicious "killing frost" (a phrase he coins)—an evil force of nature rather than the doings of divine Providence. In his despair, he will revealingly compare himself to Lucifer (line 371), the archetype of the ambitious spirit, and the first to be thrown out of a court.

Lord, What Fools These Mortals Be

PUCK: Captain of our fairy band,
    Helena is here at hand,
    And the youth, mistook by me,
    Pleading for a lover's fee.
    Shall we their fond pageant see?
    Lord, what fools these mortals be!

A MIDSUMMER NIGHT'S DREAM Act 3, scene 2, 110–115

The mischievous fairy Puck brings his king Oberon to view a spectacle—what he calls a "fond [foolish] pageant." Four Athenian lovers, lost in the fairies' forest, have lately been acting very strangely, and Puck is partly responsible. Where Oberon had hoped to reconcile, with the aid of a love potion, the bickering lovers, Puck applied the potion to the eyelids of the wrong man. Before, Helena had pursued Demetrius, who had pursued Hermia, who was in love with Lysander. Now, because of Puck's mistake, Lysander pursues Helena, and in the meanwhile Oberon has fixed it so that Demetrius pursues Helena too—the result he originally intended.

All this fairy meddling doesn't prevent Puck from blaming the lovers' behavior on their own foolishness. As far as he's concerned, their actions amount merely to a performance put on for the fairies' enjoyment, while the lovers themselves treat the whole affair with deadly seriousness. Shakespeare's judgment seems to be that love is a form of madness that prompts the lover to act in very foolish ways, indeed. As Duke Theseus says, lovers, like madmen and poets, are fantasists, "of imagination all compact [composed]" (Act 5, scene 1, 8). Though their fantasies are irrational, however, they are also acts of creation that produce "More than cool reason ever comprehends" (line 6). Theseus doesn't wholly approve of the frantic delusions of lovers and poets, but the poet Shakespeare is implicitly more tolerant.

They Did Make Love to This Employment

HORATIO: So Guildenstern and Rosencrantz go to't.
HAMLET: Why, man, they did make love to this employment,
They are not near my conscience. Their defeat
Does by their own insinuation grow.
'Tis dangerous when the baser nature comes
Between the pass and fell incensèd points
Of mighty opposites.

HAMLET   Act 5, scene 2, 56–62

King Claudius has been "hoist with his own petard" [*see* p. 57], and his unwitting agents Rosencrantz and Guildenstern have suffered the fate the king had intended for Hamlet. While sailing to England, Hamlet discovered that a letter his two friends had brought along demanded—though they didn't know it—that Hamlet be executed. Hamlet sabotages the letter and, after a brief encounter with some pirates, sends Rosencrantz, Guildenstern, and a letter commanding their execution off to England, while Hamlet returns to Denmark.

For this deadly trick Hamlet feels no remorse; his supposed "friends" had welcomed the opportunity to do King Claudius some service. By their own "insinuation" (their sneaky insertion into the King's favor), they brought doom upon themselves, even if they never understood their real roles in the king's plot. "They did make love to this employment," Hamlet announces, perhaps overemphasizing the passion with which they undertook their treachery. They were, he goes on, in over their heads; their "baser nature" (inferior quality and intelligence) could not withstand the "pass" (fencing thrust) and "fell" (fierce), incensed foil-point jabs of mighty "opposites" (opponents)—Claudius and Hamlet. The image—of Rosencrantz and Guildenstern haplessly trapped between two more powerful men engaged in a deadly fencing match—is pretty ironic. Hamlet himself, as well as almost everyone else of importance, will soon be felled by a poisoned point and poisoned pearls [*see* A HIT, A VERY PALPABLE HIT].

Make Mad the Guilty, and Appall the Free

HAMLET: O, what a rogue and peasant slave am I!
      Is it not monstrous that this player here,
      But in a fiction, in a dream of passion,
      Could force his soul so to his own conceit
      That from her working all the visage wann'd,
      Tears in his eyes, distraction in his aspect,
      A broken voice, an' his whole function suiting
      With forms to his conceit? And all for nothing,
      For Hecuba!
      What's Hecuba to him, or he to Hecuba,
      That he should weep for her? What would he do
      Had he the motive and the cue for passion
      That I have? He would drown the stage with tears,
      And cleave the general ear with horrid speech,
      Make mad the guilty, and appall the free,
      Confound the ignorant, and amaze indeed
      The very faculties of eyes and ears.

HAMLET **Act 2, scene 2, 550–566**

Hamlet is disgusted with his lackadaisical performance as an avenger. Having just heard an actor's impassioned recitation of the fall of Troy, the prince marvels that such feeling could be mustered for Hecuba, the Trojan queen, a mere indifferent fiction. The teary delivery, the actor's feigned distress, his artificial pallor—"all for nothing,/ For Hecuba!" If the actor had the very real material Hamlet has—a fratricidal stepfather, an incestuous mother, a flock of spies scrutinizing his every move —his performance would profoundly affect ("amaze indeed") a terror-stricken audience and expose the guilty party by its very force [see THE PLAY'S THE THING].

Yet despite all his "motives" and "cues," Hamlet's acting style has been rather cerebral, except when he lets loose in soliloquies like this one. Preferring cunning to rant, Hamlet instinctively distrusts histrionic display—even when it is "real" it will seem affected [see THAT WITHIN WHICH PASSES SHOW and HOLD A MIRROR UP TO NATURE].

The Makings of

3RD GENTLEMAN: At length her grace rose, and with modest paces
Came to the altar, where she kneel'd, and saint-like
Cast her fair eyes to heaven, and pray'd devoutly;
Then rose again and bow'd her to the people;
When by the archbishop of Canterbury
She had all the royal makings of a queen,
As holy oil, Edward Confessor's crown,
The rod, and bird of peace, and all such emblems
Laid nobly on her. . . .

HENRY THE EIGHTH Act 4, scene 1, 82–90

The "3rd gentleman" (Shakespeare's generic or "everyman" characters are identified by number) describes the coronation of Henry VIII's second wife, Anne Boleyn. The elaborate rituals he describes are of some historical interest; but for our purposes, what's notable is that this is the first recorded use of the phrase "the makings of." We mean "the potential to be" or "the stuff of"; Shakespeare means something like "the trappings of" or "the symbolic distinctions of." In the modern sense, Anne didn't really have "the makings of" a queen. Henry VIII, inspired by little more than lust, single-handedly "made" her, just as he was soon to "un-make" her with charges of, among other things, adultery. She was ultimately beheaded.

The Marriage of True Minds

Let me not to the marriage of true minds
Admit impediments. Love is not love
Which alters when it alteration finds,
Or bends with the remover to remove.
O no, it is an ever-fixèd mark
That looks on tempests and is never shaken;
It is the star to every wand'ring bark,
Whose worth's unknown, although his height be taken.

"Sonnet 116," 1–8

"The marriage of true minds" is a phrase both widely used and difficult to understand, at least in the way Shakespeare meant it. When we speak of a "marriage of the minds" we get around the problem of what "true" means. The notion of compatible intellects is certainly part of the original phrase, but in Shakespeare the word "marriage" is less neutral; he's speaking of a total relationship—both intellectual and erotic. "True minds" doesn't mean "authentic minds," but "faithful spirits"; "truth" in the Renaissance still had "fidelity" as one of its primary senses.

If you follow this point, you can see how Shakespeare gets on to the topic of constancy in love. Love really isn't love at all, he says, if it bends under circumstances or alters because the world around it is in a constant state of alteration. Love isn't an affair of convenience, but resolute, like "an ever-fixèd mark" (a seamark: some static object used to guide navigation). Like a seamark, love should weather all tempests without tribulation, serving like a star to wandering barks. The world and its lovers too are errant, and need stable principles for guidance; love is imagined as an almost external thing, beyond the shifting sensations of the lover.

Masters of Their Fates

CASSIUS: Why, man, he [Caesar] doth bestride the narrow world
　　　　 Like a colossus, and we petty men
　　　　 Walk under his huge legs, and peep about
　　　　 To find ourselves dishonorable graves.
　　　　 Men at some time are masters of their fates;
　　　　 The fault, dear Brutus, is not in our stars,
　　　　 But in ourselves, that we are underlings.

JULIUS CAESAR　Act 1, scene 2, 135–141

Cassius, prime mover of the assassination plot against Julius Caesar, here continues a speech he hopes will draw Brutus into the conspiracy. Cassius's technique is to inflate the grandeur, and therefore the threat, of Caesar's power, in contrast to the wormlike submissiveness, and therefore the dishonor, of other leading Romans. The philosophical sentiments are appropriately classical, specifically Stoic: it is man who controls his own destiny, not heavenly powers. It's not the "fault" of the "stars" that Caesar is on top and Brutus and Cassius are underlings; the fault is "in ourselves," in their own lack of resolve. Brutus has been trusting to fate to restrain his friend Caesar's ambitions, when Brutus really ought to think, like Cassius, about seizing fate for himself.

Method in the Madness

POLONIUS: What is the matter, my lord?

HAMLET: Between who?

POLONIUS: I mean, the matter that you read, my lord.

HAMLET: Slanders, sir; for the satirical rogue says here that old men
　　　　 have grey beards, that their faces are wrinkled, their eyes purging

thick amber and plum-tree gum, and that they have a plentiful
lack of wit, together with most weak hams; all which, sir, though
I most powerfully and potently believe, yet I hold it not honesty
to have it thus set down, for yourself, sir, shall grow old as I am, if
like a crab you could go backward.

POLONIUS: [*Aside*] Though this be madness, yet there is method in't.

HAMLET **Act 2, scene 2, 193–206**

Our expression, "There's a method in the madness," derives
from this comical scene, although we've tampered a bit with
the phrasing [*compare* THE BETTER PART OF VALOR IS DISCRE-
TION]. The politic Polonius, convinced that Hamlet is truly
mad, nonetheless recognizes in his speech some "method"—
that is, a kind of artfulness and order. Whether he appreciates
Hamlet's point is unclear.

Polonius diagnoses Hamlet's madness as a form of "love-
melancholy," considered a full-fledged disease in the Renaissance. The old man has ordered his daughter Ophelia, Hamlet's girlfriend, to refuse to see the prince or receive his letters,
and Polonius now concludes that such refusals have resulted in
Hamlet's sorry state. Hamlet, however, only puts on a show
[*see* ANTIC DISPOSITION].

As a sort of revenge on Polonius, whom he recognizes as one
of King Claudius's numerous spies, Hamlet plays the "satirical
rogue" and enumerates the debilities of age, pointedly making
fun of Polonius. In the process he borrows one of Polonius's
own rhetorical tricks: *occupatio*, or *paralepsis*—pretending to
pass over or contemn something while actually stating it openly
[*see* MORE MATTER WITH LESS ART].

The Milk of Human Kindness

LADY MACBETH: Glamis thou art, and Cawdor, and shalt be
What thou art promis'd. Yet do I fear thy nature,
It is too full o' th' milk of human kindness
To catch the nearest way.

MACBETH Act 1, scene 5, 15–18

To Lady Macbeth, the "milk of human kindness" is distasteful stuff—no self-respecting man has any use for it. Therefore, when we use the phrase to approve someone's compassion, we reverse the original sentiment.

Lady Macbeth is ambitious, and fears that her milky husband lacks the mettle to grab the Scottish crown in the most expeditious manner. "The nearest way," as she sees it, is to murder King Duncan. She hatches this plot—which had independently occurred to Macbeth as well—when he writes home that three witches have prophesied that he would be created "thane" (lord) of Cawdor, and later would ascend the throne.

The first half of the prophecy has already come true, and Lady Macbeth is in a hurry to make sure the second half comes true too.

As fluids go, Lady Macbeth is more inclined to murderous blood than nurturing milk. Later, goading the hesitant Macbeth, she insists that, if she had sworn to do it, she wouldn't have hesitated to take her own baby "while it was smiling in my face" and to "Have pluck'd my nipple from his boneless gums,/ And dash'd the brains out." A charming woman.

In My Mind's Eye

HAMLET: My father—methinks I see my father—
HORATIO: Where, my lord?
HAMLET: In my mind's eye, Horatio.
HORATIO: I saw him once, 'a was a goodly king.
HAMLET: 'A was a man, take him for all in all,
         I shall not look upon his like again.
HORATIO: My lord, I think I saw him yesternight.
HAMLET: Saw? who?
HORATIO: My lord, the King your father.

HAMLET Act 1, scene 2, 184–191.

Hamlet has the most active imagination of all Shakespeare's characters. That he coined the phrase "In my mind's eye" is therefore not surprising—his inner life is vivid, and he surveys it often.

But Hamlet's coinage *does* come as a surprise to his level-headed but shaken school chum Horatio. In the first scene of the play, the skeptical Horatio beheld, or thinks he beheld, the ghost of the former king, Hamlet's father. Hamlet's wistful "methinks I see my father" therefore unnerves his friend, whom a producer should probably instruct to whirl about to look for the ghost. Then Horatio, after assenting to Hamlet's idealizing assessment of his father's uniqueness, must break the unsettling news that Hamlet may indeed look upon his "like" again. Hamlet does, two scenes later.

A Ministering Angel

DOCTOR: No more be done:
We should profane the service of the dead
To sing a requiem and such rest to her
As to peace-parted souls.
LAERTES: Lay her i' th' earth,
And from her fair and unpolluted flesh
May violets spring! I tell thee, churlish priest,
A minist'ring angel shall my sister be
When thou liest howling.

HAMLET   Act 5, scene 1, 235–242

Laertes' sister Ophelia seems to have committed suicide; at least, the evidence is ambiguous enough to prevent the doctor of divinity from administering burial rites. Suicides were not to be accorded the same "service of the dead" as "peace-parted souls," that is, persons who peacefully allow God to determine when they should shuffle off this mortal coil. Laertes, who feeds on abstractions such as valor and purity, is indignant. Though he cannot get his sister the burial service he wishes for her, he can lash out at the "churlish priest." Have it your way, he says, but while you, Doctor, burn in hell, my sister will have been transformed into a "minist'ring angel."

In the standard sixteenth century translation of the New Testament, St. Paul informed the Hebrews that angels were "minist'ring spretes [spirits]" (1:14)—that is, ministers of God to those whose souls shall be saved. Supposedly, Ophelia, as a ministering angel, will attend to idealists like Laertes, who appreciated her unpolluted, virginal virtue, while hair-splitting priests burn.

More Honored in the Breach

[A *flourish of trumpets, and two pieces goes off*]

HORATIO: What does this mean, my lord?

HAMLET: The King doth wake to-night and takes his rouse,
Keeps wassail, and the swagg'ring up-spring reels;
And as he drains his draughts of Rhenish down,
The kettle-drum and trumpet thus bray out
The triumph of his pledge.
                                        Is it a custom?

HAMLET: Ay, marry, is't,
But to my mind, though I am native here

And to the manner born, it is a custom
More honor'd in the breach than the observance.

HAMLET Act 1, scene 4, 7–16

TO THE MANNER BORN

Outside the castle with Hamlet, nervously anticipating the reappearance of a ghost, Horatio is startled by a flourish of trumpets and the firing of cannons. Hamlet contemptuously explains the uproar as merely accompaniment to King Claudius's drunken toasts ("pledges") over Rhenish wine.

But it isn't only the king's custom to revel and carouse (to take his "rouse" and keep "wassail") late a-nights; it's the national custom, the "manner" of the people. Hamlet has adopted the English view: Danes, and Dutchmen, are regularly portrayed in Renaissance drama as constitutional soakers. Where Shakespeare seems amused, Hamlet is disgusted. The prince finds the manner to which he was born dishonorable, a national blight. Since Hamlet coined it, the phrase has come to refer to the manner not of a people but of a class—especially of the upper class. "Manner" is nearly a synonym of "manners," and what was to Hamlet's mind an insult has become a badge of distinction. I'm reminded of the British situation comedy, *To the Manor Born.*

Since, to Hamlet's mind, native customs ought to bring honor on a people, it would be more honorable to forego wassail and "up-spring reels." These customs are, as he puts it, "more honor'd in the breach than in the observance"—breaking tradition is in this case more honorable than observing it. His words have since been twisted around. Today we mean something like "more often disregarded than adhered to," perhaps taking "honor'd" to mean "observed" (as one "honors" tradition or "honors" a contract). But Hamlet's point is that the custom is observed too often, denigrating its observers rather than conferring honor on them.

More in Sorrow than in Anger

HAMLET: Then saw you not his face.
HORATIO: O yes, my lord, he wore his beaver up.
HAMLET: What, look'd he frowningly?
HORATIO: A countenance more
In sorrow than in anger.

HAMLET   Act 1, scene 2, 229–232

There's been a ghost prowling around outside the castle at Elsinore, and Hamlet's friend Horatio has gotten a good look at him. The ghost hasn't been wearing a rodent around his face, as Horatio's description might suggest: he wore his "beaver" (the visor of his helmet) raised, so Horatio recognized the host as Hamlet's father, and noted his expression. Horatio uses "more in sorrow than in anger" as an adjectival phrase, to describe a thing (a face); we use it, and its like, as an adverbial phrase, to describe an action ("She did such-and-such more in sorrow than in anger"). Either way, someone we expect to be furious (and it's not clear why Horatio should expect this) manifests a disarming sadness. When the ghost finally appears to Hamlet, however, his anger pretty much blots out his sorrow.

More Matter with Less Art

POLONIUS: Your noble son is mad:
Mad call I it, for to define true madness,
What is't but to be nothing else but mad?
But let that go.
QUEEN: More matter with less art.
POLONIUS: Madam, I swear I use no art at all.
That he's mad, 'tis true, 'tis true 'tis pity,
And pity 'tis 'tis true—a foolish figure,
But farewell it, for I will use no art.

HAMLET   Act 2, scene 2, 92–99

In one of the funniest scenes in *Hamlet*, the politician Polonius, who has declared that "Brevity is the soul of wit" [see p. 17], continues to enlarge upon Hamlet's supposed madness. The impatient Queen dryly demands "More matter with less art," that is, more substance and less rhetoric.

In Shakespeare's age, rhetoric was an element of the so-called "trivium" (grammar, rhetoric, logic) into which every schoolchild was indoctrinated. Highly rhetorical, sometimes pedantic literature had been extremely popular throughout the late sixteenth century. But by the time of *Hamlet*, Polonius's brand of "art" had begun to seem affected, passé, almost vulgar; there was a new insistence on the value of spontaneity.

Polonius, despite his protests, is anything but spontaneous.

By claiming that he uses "no art," he pretends that polished rhetoric comes as naturally to him as breathing. His tautologies and "figures"—rhetorical devices, such as chiasmus (inversion of word order), *occupatio* (pretending to pass over something one actually mentions), and parallel clauses—are, however, blatantly affected, as befits his character. Polonius, a self-satisfied, tedious old man straight out of classical comedy, tries so hard to please that he becomes annoying.

More Sinned against than Sinning

LEAR: Close pent-up guilts,
    Rive your concealing continents, and cry
    These dreadful summoners grace. I am a man
    More sinn'd against than sinning.

KING LEAR   Act 3, scene 2, 57–60

Thrown out of doors by his own daughters, the anguished Lear cries upon the storming heavens to execute justice, since he is now powerless to do so. Having ceded his authority, and been betrayed for it, the king comes to realize that he is but a "poor, infirm, weak, and despis'd old man" (line 20). As the storm beats down on his naked head, he invokes the "dreadful summoners"—the gods who tend to judgment and retribution—but hastily adds that he is himself "More sinn'd against than sinning." In this pathetic moment, Lear exemplifies in the extreme a possessive parent with ungrateful children, as he chalks up their transgressions on a cosmic balance sheet. The storm seems a manifestation of his fury, and—still clinging to the royal imperative—Lear commands it to strike where he, being weak, cannot.

More than Kin and Less than Kind

KING: But now, my cousin Hamlet, and my son—
HAMLET: A little more than kin, and less than kind.
KING: How is it that the clouds still hang on you?
HAMLET: Not so, my lord, I am too much in the sun.

HAMLET Act 1, scene 2, 64–67

"A little more than kin, and less than kind" is Prince Hamlet's withering assessment of his relationship to the new king of Denmark, his uncle Claudius. Claudius—who has secretly poisoned Hamlet's father—sleazily ingratiates himself to the mourning prince with rhetorical appellatives like "my cousin Hamlet, and my son." ("Cousin" in Renaissance English could refer to an aunt, uncle, niece, or nephew.) Hamlet mutters that Claudius is more than "kin" (more than a "cousin" because now a stepfather), but definitely less than "kind."

"Kind" has a triple meaning here, as often in Shakespeare [see THE MOST UNKINDEST CUT OF ALL]. On one hand, Hamlet says that Claudius is less than a direct blood relative, "kind" meaning "ancestral stock." On another hand, Hamlet refers to what he sees as Claudius's unnatural lust, "kind" meaning "natural." Finally, Hamlet indicates his resentment toward the new king for his insensitive haste in marrying the queen. Here, "kind" has it's modern sense: "considerate."

Hamlet pushes the black humor further in responding to Claudius's reproachful comment on his clouded disposition. "I am too much in the sun" plays on the sun/son pun which an audience could not miss.

The Multitudinous Seas Incarnadine

[*Knocking within*]

MACBETH: Whence is that knocking?
How is't with me, when every noise appalls me?
What hands are here? Hah! They pluck out mine eyes.
Will all great Neptune's ocean wash this blood
Clean from my hand? No; this my hand will rather
The multitudinous seas incarnadine,
Making the green one red.

MACBETH **Act 2, scene 2, 54–60**

"The multitudinous seas incarnadine" is understandably confusing to modern readers, but Macbeth explains his meaning in the following line. Shakespeare makes a verb out of "incarnadine," a sixteenth century adjective meaning "pink." (The Latin root *carn-* refers to flesh, and thus, in its derivatives, to flesh color.) "To incarnadine" is thus to turn something pink or light red—what Macbeth imagines his bloody hands will do to Neptune's green ocean [*see* A SORRY SIGHT]. After Shakespeare, the verb and adjective have both come to refer to the color of blood itself—crimson—rather than to the light red of a bloodied sea.

Macbeth has come to recognize that his guilt can never be washed off, even if the blood can be washed from his hands. Instead, his guilt will poison the world around him, which he compares to an ocean. He has already begun to hallucinate: here, he imagines hands plucking out his eyes in retribution for the murder of Duncan.

If Music Be the Food of Love, Play On

DUKE ORSINO: If music be the food of love, play on,
              Give me excess of it; that surfeiting,
              The appetite may sicken, and so die.

TWELFTH NIGHT   Act 1, scene 1, 1–3

Duke Orsino of Illyria, presiding over the merry, mixed-up world of *Twelfth Night,* opens the play with these festive sentiments, soured though they be by the affected airs of the melancholic lover. He has convinced himself that he's insanely in love with a wealthy and resistant lady, who is in mourning for her brother and only annoyed by Orsino's inappropriate attentions. The duke's idea of a cure for his disease is to stuff himself sick with his own passions.

Orsino's brand of self-indulgent pouting comes in for much ribbing here and elsewhere in Shakespeare, most vividly in *As You Like It* and *Much Ado about Nothing.* For melancholic poseurs like Orsino, who are actually expected to make spectacles of themselves, affecting gestures are more important than sincere emotions.

Neither a Borrower nor a Lender Be

POLONIUS: Neither a borrower nor a lender be,
For loan oft loses both itself and friend,
And borrowing dulls the edge of husbandry.

HAMLET   Act 1, scene 3, 75–77

Old Polonius counsels his hotheaded son Laertes, who is about to embark for Paris for his gentleman's education [*see* THE PRIM-ROSE PATH]. While he still has the chance, Polonius wholesales a stockroom of aphorisms, the most famous of which is "Neither a borrower nor a lender be."

On Polonius's terms, there is little to argue with in his perhaps ungenerous advice. His logic is thus: lending money to friends is risky, because hitching debt onto personal relationships can cause resentment and, in the case of default, loses the lender both his money and his friend. Borrowing invites more private dangers: it supplants domestic thrift ("husbandry")—in Polonius's eyes, an important gentlemanly value.

Incidentally, in the days when *Hamlet* was first staged, borrowing was epidemic among the gentry, who sometimes neglected husbandry to the point where they were selling off their estates piece by piece to maintain an ostentatious lifestyle in London.

There Was Never Yet Philosopher that Could Endure the Toothache Patiently

LEONATO: Therefore give me no counsel,
My griefs cry louder than advertisement.
ANTONIO: Therein do men from children nothing differ.

LEONATO: I pray thee peace, I will be flesh and blood;
For there was never yet philosopher
That could endure the toothache patiently,
However they have writ the style of gods,
And made a push at chance and sufferance.

MUCH ADO ABOUT NOTHING   Act 5, scene 1, 31–38

Debating with his brother the merits of stoic endurance, Leonato scoffs. Having watched as his daughter was accused by her fiancé, on the morning of her wedding, of fornication; having had his own honor thus indirectly besmirched; having been taken in by the accusations and then having threatened his daughter; and after she has nearly died of shame, Leonato is in no mood to forgive and forget. Antonio insists that it is childish to indulge in grief and self-pity. Leonato retorts that however much even philosophers might pretend to godlike detachment from the pains and passions of life, they nonetheless howl when they've got a toothache.

Obscurely, Leonato sneers at the philosophers' having "made a push at chance and sufferance"; "push" could either be a form of "pish"—a scornful dismissal, as in "pish-posh"— or could mean "counterattack, resistance." While stoics disdain the reversals of chance and the gnawings of "sufferance" (suffering), they're really just using highfalutin language to fool themselves.

The Noblest Roman of Them All

MARCUS ANTONIUS: This was the noblest Roman of them all:
All the conspirators, save only he,
Did that they did in envy of great Caesar;
He, only in a general honest thought
And common good to all, made one of them.

JULIUS CAESAR Act 5, scene 5, 68–72

The noblest Roman of them all, according to Marc Antony, was Brutus—one of Caesar's assassins, and now a corpse at Antony's feet. The note of regret here is ironic, to say the least, because Antony raised the army which has destroyed Brutus.

Yet Antony now comes to praise Brutus, not to bury him. Of all the conspirators, only Brutus thought of the "common good," and had honest intentions toward the general populace [see THE SERPENT'S EGG]. The rest merely envied Caesar's greatness; Brutus thought it a real threat to the Republic.

Antony's words once again reveal his penchant for superlatives. "The noblest Roman of them all" directly echoes "The most unkindest cut of all" [see p. 173]. In effect, he paints Brutus, at different times, both as a superlative villain and as a superlative Roman. In both cases, Antony is supremely aware of the rhetorical necessities of the situation.

Nothing Either Good or Bad, but Thinking Makes It So

HAMLET: What have you, my good friends, deserv'd at the hands of Fortune, that she sends you to prison hither?

GUILDENSTERN: Prison, my lord?

HAMLET: Denmark's a prison.

ROSENCRANTZ: Then is the world one.

HAMLET: A goodly one, in which there are many confines, wards, and dungeons, Denmark being one o' th' worst.

ROSENCRANTZ: We think not so, my lord.

HAMLET: Why then 'tis none to you; for there is nothing either good or bad, but thinking makes it so. To me it is a prison.

HAMLET Act 2, scene 2, 239–251

What brings Rosencrantz and Guildenstern—two of Hamlet's acquaintances from the university—to Denmark isn't Lady Fortune but, as Hamlet suspects, King Claudius. Claudius is worried about Hamlet's seeming distraction, thinking it might be a threat to the state and to the king himself. Claudius coerces Rosencrantz and Guildenstern, who aren't too bright, into service as spies, hoping they can lull the prince into revealing the true cause of his "antic disposition" [see p. 2].

When Hamlet calls Denmark a prison, therefore, the metaphor is apt. He is mentally and physically confined by the gaze of the king and his agents, and he feels trapped in the court's general degradation—"Something is rotten in the state of Denmark," as Marcellus had said [see p. 135].

Hamlet is a prisoner of his own thinking, and of his knowledge that his stepfather is a fratricide and his mother incestuous. When he states that "there is nothing either good or bad, but thinking makes it so," he's not indulging in ethical relativism as much as wishing for blissful ignorance. He's also implicitly damning the naïveté of the king's new yes-men.

Nothing in His Life Became Him like the Leaving It

KING DUNCAN: Is execution done on Cawdor? Are not
               Those in commission yet return'd?
MALCOLM: My liege,
               They are not yet come back. But I have spoke
               With one that saw him die; who did report
               That very frankly he confess'd his treasons,
               Implor'd your Highness' pardon, and set forth
               A deep repentance. Nothing in his life
               Became him like the leaving it.

                              MACBETH Act 1, scene 4, 1–8

The traitorous Thane (lord) of Cawdor, who had taken part in Norwegian campaigns against his own king, Duncan of Scotland, is here reported executed for his treason. This is quite convenient for the valorous Macbeth, who thus inherits the former thane's title, as the three witches had predicted [see THE MILK OF HUMAN KINDNESS and CHANCE MAY CROWN ME].

Malcolm, one of the king's two sons, pictures the erstwhile Cawdor's histrionic repentance at the gallows. "Nothing in his life," moralizes Malcolm, "became him" (reflected as well on his character) like his pious loyalty on the verge of execution.

Shakespeare's audience did not have to strain their imaginations to visualize the scene; the same sort of spectacle was not unknown early in the reign of King James. James delighted in such groveling mea culpas, but unlike Duncan sometimes rewarded the groveler with his life.

Once More unto the Breach

KING HENRY: Once more unto the breach, dear friends, once more;
Or close the wall up with our English dead.
In peace there's nothing so becomes a man
As modest stillness and humility;
But when the blast of war blows in our ears,
Then imitate the action of the tiger. . . .

HENRY THE FIFTH Act 3, scene 1, 1–6

On rather debatable pretexts, King Henry V has led an army —he calls them "dear friends"—over the channel to invade France. This speech typifies Henry's rousing oratory, as he ex-

ploits his personal popularity and his men's notions of masculinity. Disclaiming responsibility for the invasion—the blast of war blows but no one seems to blow it—he nevertheless takes charge with his royal directives, of which "Once more unto the breach" is the most famous. As Henry's army batters the fortifying walls around the port town of Harfleur, the king urges them to pound again and again, and to rush again and again at the break in the wall. Failing successful entry to the town, his "tigers" should clog up the breach with their dead bodies—to form, one supposes, a blockade. The heartened troops rally behind their leader.

One Fell Swoop

MALCOLM: Be comforted.
                Let's make us med'cines of our great revenge
                To cure this deadly grief.
MACDUFF: He has no children.—All my pretty ones?
                Did you say all?—O hell-kite!—All?
                What, all my pretty chickens, and their dam,
                At one fell swoop?

                                    MACBETH   Act 4, scene 3, 213–219

We employ "fell" almost exclusively as the past tense of "fall," and occasionally as a verb in its own right, meaning "to cut down." Macduff uses "fell" in a sense that is now rare—as an adjective meaning "fierce, deadly." King Macbeth, who knows that Macduff is conspiring to overthrow him, had ordered the murder of Macduff's wife, children, and servants. This is the "fell swoop": Macduff likens Macbeth to a "hell-kite" (the kite is a vicious bird of prey in the falcon family). While Macduff's poultry metaphor has not worn well, the phrase "one fell swoop" has become a regular part of the language. Part of its appeal, besides its evocative sound, is its economic phrasing, which suggests all three meanings of "fell": Macbeth figuratively "falls" from the sky in a "fierce, deadly" swoop to "cut down" Macduff's family.

One May Smile, and Smile, and Be a Villain

HAMLET: O most pernicious woman!
   O villain, villain, smiling, damnèd villain!
   My tables—meet it is I set it down
   That one may smile, and smile, and be a villain—
   At least I am sure it may be so in Denmark.

HAMLET Act 1, scene 5, 105–109

Hamlet has just encountered for the first time the ghost of his father, who was, as he tells his son, poisoned by his own brother Claudius (the "smiling, damnèd villain"). Claudius then grabbed both the old king's crown and his queen—Hamlet's mother, that "pernicious woman."

The ghost, like Hamlet, assesses the queen's remarriage as

"luxury and damnèd incest" (line 83). But he asks Hamlet to let heaven punish that crime; his son's job is to take revenge on Claudius. And though Hamlet's spite is directed first at his mother [see FRAILTY, THY NAME IS WOMAN], here he lingers lovingly on the usurper's treachery.

We've briefly encountered the new king's unctuous rhetoric in earlier scenes [see MORE THAN KIN AND LESS THAN KIND]. Hamlet hated it from the start, but now that he knows about Claudius's fratricide, distaste has become perverse fascination. He pulls out his "tables" (a writing tablet) to note down that one may "smile, and smile, and be a villain." In Shakespeare's previous tragedy, *Julius Caesar*, the young Octavius delivered the working version of Hamlet's aphorism: "And some that smile have in their hearts, I fear,/ Millions of mischiefs" (Act 4, scene 1, 50–51).

One that Loved Not Wisely but Too Well

OTHELLO: I pray you, in your letters,
When you shall these unlucky deeds relate,
Speak of me as I am; nothing extenuate,
Nor set down aught in malice. Then must you speak
Of one that lov'd not wisely but too well;
Of one not easily jealous, but being wrought,
Perplex'd in the extreme. . . .

OTHELLO   Act 5, scene 2, 340–346

This is Othello's swan song: his attempt, before killing himself, to justify having suffocated his blameless wife Desdemona. The solidity of this speech reveals one side of Othello's personality —calm, cool, and collected. But the fact that Othello seems to have recovered from the jealous passion that drove him to murder his wife doesn't ensure his credibility. Some readers, pitying the Moor's anguish, wish to accept his self-judgment— that he may not have loved in the wisest fashion, but he loved very deeply, and that is the reason he was "Perplex'd in the extreme" by groundless charges against Desdemona.

Others, unable to forgive Othello's rash, brutal, and over-confident act, find his justification just another self-delusion. In fact, Othello has shown himself extremely susceptible to jealousy. And it is difficult to accept that his foolish credulous-ness is compatible with loving his wife too well—he never gave her the benefit of the doubt or any real chance to defend herself.

Out, Damned Spot

DOCTOR: What is it she does now? Look how she rubs her hands.

GENTLEWOMAN: It is an accustom'd action with her, to seem thus washing her hands. I have known her continue in this a quarter of an hour.

LADY MACBETH: Yet here's a spot.

DOCTOR: Hark, she speaks. I will set down what comes from her, to satisfy my remembrance the more strongly.

LADY MACBETH: Out, damn'd spot! out, I say!—One; two: why, then 'tis time to do't.—Hell is murky.—Fie, my lord, fie, a soldier, and afeard? What need we fear who knows it, when none can call our pow'r to accompt?—Yet who would have thought the old man to have had so much blood in him?

MACBETH Act 5, scene 1, 26–40

Lady Macbeth, as has become her wont, sleepwalks through the royal castle. As her waiting-woman and her doctor listen in, she mutters fragments of an imaginary conversation that recalls the night she and her husband conspired to murder King Duncan [see A SORRY SIGHT]. The hour is two o'clock; she upbraids her husband for his bad conscience; she insists that there will be nothing to fear once they've grabbed the crown; she marvels at how much blood Duncan had to shed. As Lady Macbeth replays this scene for the eavesdroppers, she not only incriminates herself, but also reveals the pangs of conscience she had ridiculed in her husband.

"Out, damn'd spot" is a prime example of "Instant Bard," tailor-made for ironic jokes and marketing schemes. But the "spot" isn't a coffee stain, it's blood. One motif of *Macbeth* is how tough it is to wash, scrub, or soak out nasty bloodstains. Macbeth had said that even the ocean couldn't wash his hands clean of Duncan's blood; Lady Macbeth, who scorned him then, now finds the blood dyed into her conscience. The king and queen persist in imagining that physical actions can root out psychological demons, but the play is an exposition of how wrong they are.

A Pair of Star-Crossed Lovers

CHORUS: Two households, both alike in dignity,
        In fair Verona, where we lay our scene,
        From ancient grudge break to new mutiny,
        Where civil blood makes civil hands unclean.
        From forth the fatal loins of these two foes
        A pair of star-cross'd lovers take their life;
        Whose misadventur'd piteous overthrows
        Doth with their death bury their parents' strife.

                     ROMEO AND JULIET Prologue, 1–8

In a sonnet no one would claim as Shakespeare's best, the chorus reports a feud between two families "alike in dignity" (of equal social rank), the Montagues and Capulets. Romeo, a Montague, and Juliet, a Capulet, are the "pair of star-cross'd lovers" whose misadventures and deaths will finally put an end to the feud. "Star-cross'd" means "opposed (crossed) by the stars," the arbiters of man's fate. As sophisticated as Renaissance thought was in many ways, the Copernican revolution had yet to have much of an impact. It was still popularly believed that the celestial order directly affected the affairs of the world.

Romeo and Juliet, only the second of Shakespeare's ten tragedies, relies heavily on the rhetoric and devices of the classical tragedies Renaissance dramatists used as models. A prologue delivered by a chorus is one such device; and, as prologues generally did, this one lays out the "argument" (plot and moral) of the play. Suspense was not important to the audiences who came to see *Romeo and Juliet*—most of them would already have known the story anyway.

Parting is Such Sweet Sorrow

JULIET: 'Tis almost morning, I would have thee gone—
And yet no farther than a wanton's bird,
That lets it hop a little from his hand,
Like a poor prisoner in his twisted gyves,
And with a silken thread plucks it back again,
So loving-jealous of his liberty.

ROMEO: I would I were thy bird.

JULIET: Sweet, so would I,
Yet I should kill thee with much cherishing.

Good night, good night! Parting is such sweet sorrow,
That I shall say good night till it be morrow. [*Exit above*]

ROMEO AND JULIET   Act 2, scene 2, 176–185

Depending on how gripping you find the first balcony scene in
Romeo and Juliet, Juliet's parting may or may not be "such sweet
sorrow." In any case, her phrase is an oxymoron, combining
contradictory ideas of pleasure and pain. Parting is sorrowful
because Juliet would prefer, like a mischievous youth ("wanton"), to snare her lover in twisted "gyves" (chains or fetters).
Parting is pleasurable, presumably, because doing anything
with Romeo is pleasurable. Note the latent sadomasochism of
this exchange, and the almost wistful prophecy that Romeo
will be killed with too much cherishing.

Juliet's "Good night, good night!" is, incidentally, the thou-
sand-and-first and thousand-and-second times she bids Romeo
goodnight [*see* A THOUSAND TIMES GOOD NIGHT].

Passing Strange

OTHELLO: My story being done,
        She gave me for my pains a world of sighs;
        She swore, in faith 'twas strange, 'twas passing strange;
        'Twas pitiful, 'twas wondrous pitiful.
        She wish'd she had not heard it, yet she wish'd
        That heaven had made her such a man.

OTHELLO   Act 1, scene 3, 158–163

"Passing strange," a phrase currently enjoying a comeback,
means "surpassingly strange"—stranger than strange. "Passing"

was often used adverbially in the Renaissance, which had a keen sense of the superlative in human achievement. The passing strangeness of Othello's tales of "hair-breadth scapes i' th' imminent deadly breach" (line 136) conjures up, like tragedy, pity and fear, and also desire.

Othello, who has been accused of seducing Desdemona with drugs and charms, is explaining how he wooed her, not with narcotics, but with anecdotes [see A ROUND UNVARNISHED TALE]. Othello's romantic, exploit-filled life—especially as he poetically enhances it—*does* act like a sort of charm on Desdemona, who can't get enough of Othello's varnished tales. Hearing of what he calls the "dangers I had pass'd" (line 167), Desdemona utters the response Othello quotes here.

Desdemona's wish that "heaven had made her such a man" is, though Othello doesn't notice, strangely ambiguous. Desdemona may be wishing heaven had sent her a husband just like Othello—this is Othello's reading; or perhaps she wishes that heaven had made her a swashbuckling man rather than a cloistered woman. In either case, marriage to the Moor becomes an escape from the confined, unromantic life of a senator's daughter.

The Patient Must Minister to Himself

MACBETH: Canst thou not minister to a mind diseas'd,
Pluck from the memory a rooted sorrow,
Raze out the written troubles of the brain,
And with some sweet oblivious antidote
Cleanse the stuff'd bosom of that perilous stuff
Which weighs upon the heart?

DOCTOR: Therein the patient
        Must minister to himself.
MACBETH: Throw physic to the dogs, I'll none of it.

MACBETH   Act 5, scene 3, 40–47

A doctor has been called in to treat the sleepwalking Lady Macbeth, queen of Scotland [*see* OUT, DAMNED SPOT]. Macbeth, recognizing his wife's severe case of guilty conscience, asks the doctor whether he can't do something about it. As the doctor well knows, but Macbeth and his wife have trouble acknowledging, a physician cannot treat one's conscience with the same medicine he uses to heal the body. "Therein," says the doctor, "the patient/ Must minister to himself"—in other words, "that's your own problem." With characteristically brutal abandon, Macbeth scorns all "physic" (medicine)—it's sour grapes to him. Self-ministration of the spiritual variety is hardly his style. Macbeth will suit up in his armor and put the sword to his enemies, treating them as if they were his disease, and as if routing them were the cure for his guilt.

What a Piece of Work Is A Man

HAMLET: What a piece of work is a man, how noble in reason, how
    infinite in faculties, in form and moving how express and
    admirable, in action how like an angel, in apprehension how like
    a god! the beauty of the world, the paragon of animals—and yet,
    to me, what is this quintessence of dust? Man delights not me—
    nor woman neither, though by your smiling you seem to say so.
ROSENCRANTZ: My lord, there was no such stuff in my thoughts.

HAMLET   Act 2, scene 2, 303–312

This passage has provoked bitter scholarly battles—over its

punctuation. Is Hamlet saying that man is like an angel in apprehension (understanding), or like a god in apprehension? The different placement of commas in the early texts of the play makes all the difference.

We're not going to settle the argument here; you probably get the drift of Hamlet's speech anyway. Man is the noblest of all God's pieces of work, the "quintessence of dust" (the fifth, or purest, extract from the dust of which all things are compounded). But despite the nobility, the reason, the grace, and the beauty of man, Hamlet cannot be delighted. At least, so he tells the king's parasites, Rosencrantz and Guildenstern, as he explains his melancholia. This is one of the moments where Hamlet's sincerity is genuinely in question. Like his claim that Denmark seems to him a prison [see THERE IS NOTHING EITHER GOOD OR BAD, BUT THINKING MAKES IT SO], Hamlet's disgust here seems more than an act, though perhaps he exaggerates for the benefit of the king's spies.

A Plague on Both Your Houses

ROMEO: Hold, Tybalt! Good Mercutio!
          [Tybalt under Romeo's arm thrusts Mercutio in. Away Tybalt]
MERCUTIO: I am hurt.
          A plague a' both your houses! I am sped.
          Is he gone and hath nothing?

                    ROMEO AND JULIET   Act 3, scene 1, 90–92

Mercutio's famous line might not be exactly the one Shakespeare wrote: instead of "a' both your houses," various old editions have "on your houses," "a' both the houses," "of both the houses," and "a' both houses." The line as I've given it here is merely editorial reconstruction—in other words, a good guess at what the "original" might have looked like, if there was only one original. This whole passage is muddled in the early texts, and in this it is not unique; what you read on the page of a modern edition of Shakespeare, let alone what you see at the theater, may not be what Shakespeare himself wrote. You're brushing up not only your Shakespeare, but also Shakespeare's editors.

In this confusing scene, Juliet's cousin Tybalt, peeved that Romeo had crashed a Capulet family ball, comes with sword drawn looking for the young lover and his cohorts. Romeo (now married to Juliet) at first refuses to be provoked by Tybalt, which enrages Romeo's mercurial friend Mercutio. Mercutio draws, Romeo intercedes, and Tybalt stabs Mercutio under Romeo's armpit. Mercutio, chagrined and disgusted, cries "a plague a' both your houses"—the feuding houses of Capulet and Montague—and complains that Tybalt has escaped unscathed. Shortly, after Mercutio has died and Tybalt has returned, Romeo, provoked once more, pays back the deed, kills Tybalt, and is therefore forced to flee Verona.

The Play's the Thing

HAMLET: I'll have grounds
        More relative than this—the play's the thing
        Wherein I'll catch the conscience of the King.
                              HAMLET Act 2, scene 2, 603–605

When exclaiming "The play's the thing!" we're seldom asked the embarrassing question of what "thing" we mean, exactly.

Prince Hamlet, however, has something specific in mind. To elicit visible proof of what a rather visible ghost has told him —that his uncle, King Claudius, murdered his father, the former king—the prince turns playwright. His task: to sneak a few telling lines into a play about regicide his uncle will be watching at court, and to wait for Claudius to flinch. If Hamlet's plan works, he'll be convinced of both the ghost's veracity and the king's guilt and will (theoretically) feel better about paying his uncle back in kind.

The plot is intricate and bizarre, but Hamlet is relying on good, solid Renaissance psychology. Playwrights often claimed that their work encouraged virtue in upstanding citizens and caught the conscience of malefactors. About ten years after the first production of *Hamlet*, playwright Thomas Heywood edified the reading public with this real-life tale: During the performance of a particularly gruesome tragedy, in which the actors staged the murder of a man by driving a nail through his temple, a woman in the audience rose up distractedly. She "oft sighed out these words: Oh my husband, my husband!" The woman subsequently confessed all and was burned for having murdered her spouse with "a great nail" through "the brainpan."

Pomp and Circumstance

OTHELLO: O farewell,
        Farewell the neighing steed, and the shrill trump;
        The spirit-stirring drum, th' ear-piercing fife;
        The royal banner, and all quality,
        Pride, pomp, and circumstance of glorious war!
        And O you mortal engines, whose rude throats

Th' immortal Jove's dread clamors counterfeit,
Farewell! Othello's occupation's gone.

OTHELLO   Act 3, scene 3, 350–357

If there were one speech that revealed Othello's "tragic flaw," this would be it. The noble Moor, who has led a life of astounding exploits and military glory, has ultimately staked his self-image and peace of mind on his marriage to a Venetian woman of privilege. When the villain Iago craftily persuades Othello that his wife has been unfaithful—a highly improbable event—the general bids farewell not just to marital bliss, but to his livelihood ("occupation"). No longer, he cries, can he experience "all quality,/ Pride, pomp, and circumstance of glorious war!"

Othello obviously isn't talking about his high school graduation. "Pomp and circumstance" (and "quality" and "pride") are the glories and ceremonies of warfare. In war's splendid rituals, Othello has forged his identity. Although we often use "pomp and circumstance" negatively, to denote affectation and overwrought exhibitionism, the Renaissance would have been more generous: pomp and circumstance were considered inherent, positive duties of the exalted classes.

A Pound of Flesh

SHYLOCK: Most learnèd judge, a sentence! Come prepare!
PORTIA: Tarry a little, there is something else.
This bond doth give thee here no jot of blood;
The words expressly are "a pound of flesh."

THE MERCHANT OF VENICE   Act 4, scene 1, 304–307

"A pound of flesh" is a figurative way of referring to a harsh demand or spiteful penalty—the consequences of defaulting on a desperate bargain. But the usurer Shylock demands a literal pound of flesh as security when the merchant Antonio comes to borrow money for a friend [see BATED BREATH]. It's clear that the sensational bargain, with its hint of archetypal vengeance, fascinated its first audience as it fascinates us. When the play was first published, its title page advertised "The most excellent History of the *Merchant of Venice*. With the extreme cruelty of *Shylock* the Jew towards the said merchant, in cutting a just pound of his flesh. . . ."

Clever marketing, but false advertising. It's true that Antonio agrees to Shylock's brutal terms, although he knows that the usurer despises him. But while Antonio is ultimately forced to default, and while Shylock refuses the merchant's pleas for mercy, the usurer is foiled in the end. Dressed as an eminent judge, Antonio's indirect beneficiary Portia takes Shylock's insistence on the letter of the bond to its absurd conclusion. The bond specified only a pound of *flesh*, she maintains, but "no jot of blood." Shylock may be demonic but he can't perform miracles; Portia's clever piece of legal hairsplitting carries the day.

The Primrose Path

OPHELIA: But, good my brother,
     Do not, as some ungracious pastors do,
     Show me the steep and thorny way to heaven,
     Whiles, like a puff'd and reckless libertine,
     Himself the primrose path of dalliance treads,
     And reaks not his own rede.
LAERTES: O, fear me not.

HAMLET   Act 1, scene 3, 46–51

Yes, we have Shakespeare to blame for all the confusion between "primrose path" and "garden path." Ophelia, Hamlet's sweetheart, coins the former, meaning "the path of luxury," apparently linking primroses to libertine indulgence. The primrose had, since at least the fifteenth century, been associated with the metaphorical "flower" of youth, and so, indirectly, with youthful appetites.

Here, Ophelia responds to her brother's warnings to play things cool with Hamlet. Laertes is about to depart for Paris, a city Ophelia regards as at least as corrupting as Hamlet's love, and she turns Laertes' preachings back on the preacher. Indulging in mild satire on the church, she counsels her brother to "reak his own rede" (heed his own advice) and avoid the lifestyle of a "puff'd" (arrogant), incautious libertine. She seems to accept his assurances, but her father Polonius is hardly so sanguine—he will not shy from sending a spy after his son.

Prodigious Birth

JULIET: Go ask his name.—If he be married,
My grave is like to be my wedding-bed.

NURSE: His name is Romeo, and a Montague,
The only son of your great enemy.

JULIET: My only love sprung from my only hate!
Too early seen unknown, and known too late!
Prodigious birth of love it is to me
That I must love a loathèd enemy.

ROMEO AND JULIET Act 1, scene 5, 134–141

At her father's masked ball, Juliet falls in a big way for the disguised Romeo, a Montague and thus an enemy of her family [*see* A PAIR OF STAR-CROSSED LOVERS and DANCING DAYS]. Even though she has nothing personal against the Montagues, Romeo in particular, she can't escape being a Capulet, or escape her family's "hate."

Today "prodigy" usually refers to a precocious youngster. But the word had much different connotations in Shakespeare's time: a "prodigy" was someone or something abnormal, a monstrosity. Prodigies were taken to be omens of a family's bad fortune; this idea was thus naturally linked to the idea of birth, an event surrounded with a vast structure of superstition. While the word "prodigious"—of sixteenth century origin—was often applied to newborns or children, "prodigious birth" seems to be Shakespeare's coinage. When Juliet refers to the "prodigious birth" of her love, her imagination runs through the horrors such an omen portends; with deadly dramatic irony, she foresees that her grave will in fact prove her marriage bed.

In a play contemporaneous with *Romeo and Juliet*, Shakespeare has a fairy-king bless the marriage beds of three newlywed couples. He commands that "the blots of Nature's hand/ Shall not in their issue stand;/ Never mole, hair-lip, nor scar,/ Nor mark prodigious, such as are/ Despisèd in nativity,/ Shall upon their children be" (A *Midsummer Night's Dream*, Act 5, scene 1, 409–414). This passage is an excellent rendering of Elizabethans' dread of prodigious births.

Put Money in Thy Purse

IAGO: I have profess'd me thy friend, and I confess me knit to thy
deserving with cables of perdurable toughness. I could never better
stead thee than now. Put money in thy purse; follow thou the
wars; defeat thy favor with an usurp'd beard. I say put money in
thy purse. It cannot be long that Desdemona should continue her
love to the Moor—put money in thy purse—nor he his to her.

OTHELLO   Act 1, scene 3, 336–344

Despite Iago's admission that "I am not what I am" [see HEART ON MY SLEEVE], Roderigo continues to step into all Iago's snares. Roderigo is frantically in love with Othello's wife Desdemona, a situation Iago skillfully exploits: he takes Roderigo's gifts, insisting that he's delivering them to Desdemona, while keeping them himself. Whenever Roderigo grows desperate at his lack of success, Iago has to revive the gull's impossible hopes, as he does here.

Insisting that he is bound to Roderigo by the indestructible cables of true friendship, Iago self-servingly orders his dupe to keep putting money in his purse. His other advice—to become a soldier, and to get a man's beard even if he has to get a phony one—merely marks time between the repetitions of "put money in thy purse." Iago is an absolute materialist, and—so that he may continue to line his own pockets—he frames Roderigo's prospects in material terms: there's no love that money can't buy.

The Quality of Mercy Is Not Strained

PORTIA: You stand within his danger, do you not?
ANTONIO: Ay, so he says.
PORTIA: Do you confess the bond?
ANTONIO: I do.
PORTIA: Then must the Jew be merciful.
SHYLOCK: On what compulsion must I? tell me that.
PORTIA: The quality of mercy is not strain'd,
       It droppeth as the gentle rain from heaven
       Upon the place beneath. It is twice blest:
       It blesseth him that gives and him that takes.

              THE MERCHANT OF VENICE   Act 4, scene 1, 180–187

Disguised as a doctor of law, Portia has come to rescue Antonio, the merchant of Venice. Antonio had foolishly signed a bond granting the usurer Shylock a "pound of flesh" [*see* p. 114] if he defaulted on the loan he was forced to seek—ironically, in order to help a friend court Portia. And defaulted Antonio has. After determining the facts of the case, Portia doesn't appeal at first to legal technicalities—which is the only way she will force Shylock to submit—but delivers a Christian moral. When Shylock demands to know why he "must" be merciful, Portia replies that compulsion is precisely contrary to the spirit of mercy, which is not "strain'd" (forced). Only because mercy is voluntary—because it mitigates the compulsions of the literal law—is it true mercy, which drops gently like heaven's rain, a natural and gracious quality rather than a legal one. That Portia treats her Christian ethics as natural and universal, however, raises questions about the quality of her own compassion for the Jew. In the end, only because Antonio requests some mercy for Shylock is he spared complete destitution, on the condition he convert to Christianity.

Neither Rhyme nor Reason

DROMIO: But I pray, sir, why am I beaten?

ANTIPHOLUS: Dost thou not know?

DROMIO: Nothing, sir, but that I am beaten.

ANTIPHOLUS: Shall I tell you why?

DROMIO: Ay, sir, and wherefore; for they say, every why hath a wherefore.

ANTIPHOLUS: Why, first, for flouting me, and then wherefore, for urging it the second time to me.

DROMIO: Was there ever any man thus beaten out of season,
When in the why and the wherefore is neither rhyme nor reason?

THE COMEDY OF ERRORS Act 2, scene 2, 39–48

The phrase "neither rhyme nor reason" will show up again in Shakespeare—in *As You Like It* (Act 3, scene 2) and, with variation, in *The Merry Wives of Windsor* (Act 5, scene 5). The linking of these two alliterative nouns is at least as old as the poet John Skelton, who in the 1520s wrote that "For reason can I none find/ Nor good rhyme in your matter." The phrase as we use it today, however, is first preserved in Shakespeare's earliest comedy. (The earliest citation in the *OED* is from 1664.)

The Comedy of Errors, an apprentice work, is Shakespeare's attempt to adapt Latin comedy to the English stage. In all the old comedies, masters constantly threaten to—or actually do —abuse their servants, and Shakespeare's Antipholus of Syracuse is no exception. When the servant Dromio begs for an explanation of what he's done wrong, Antipholus says that Dromio is "flouting" (mocking) him by denying having said something Antipholus is sure Dromio said. The confused Dromio, sure that he hasn't said what Antipholus thinks he said, finds "neither rhyme nor reason" in the accusation—that is, neither order nor inherent sense. The confusion, though neither knows it, is due to the existence of twin Antipholuses and Dromios; farcical episodes of mistaken identity account for the entire plot of the play.

Let Rome in Tiber Melt

CLEOPATRA: Call in the messengers. As I am Egypt's queen,
Thou blushest, Antony, and that blood of thine
Is Caesar's homager; else so thy cheek pays shame
When shrill-tongu'd Fulvia scolds. The messengers!

ANTONY: Let Rome in Tiber melt, and the wide arch
Of the rang'd empire fall! Here is my space,
Kingdoms are clay; our dungy earth alike
Feeds beast as man. . . .

ANTONY AND CLEOPATRA Act 1, scene 1, 29–36

Cleopatra, Queen of Egypt, is just a little bit possessive of her latest lover, the Roman triumvir Marc Antony. When a messenger arrives from Rome, Cleopatra promptly launches into a jealous fit. She interprets Antony's embarrassed blush as either, or both, a mark of servitude to Caesar Octavius ("homager" means "vassal") or a mark of the shame he feels when reminded of his Roman wife, Fulvia.

In the high terms that typify the lovers' language, Antony dismisses Cleopatra's charges with the famous "Let Rome in Tiber melt." Rome could dissolve into the River Tiber and he'd be unmoved, because his world is now defined by Cleopatra's presence. What is empire to him, he asks, but mere clay? What is noble in ruling over "dungy earth," which has no inherent nobility, which yields its fruits to beast as well as to man? Nobility lies in our passions, and Antony's passions reside with Cleopatra.

When a messenger later reports to Cleopatra that Antony has remarried (Fulvia had died, it turns out), the queen exclaims "Melt Egypt into Nile!" (Act 2, scene 5)—almost a parody of Antony's line. Similar images of melting abound in this play: for example, Antony's "Authority melts from me" (Act 3, scene 13) and Cleopatra's "The crown o' th' earth doth melt" (Act 4, scene 15). Antony's cry of "Let Rome in Tiber melt" and Cleopatra's "Melt Egypt into Nile" are, in a sense, translated into events—not the fall of empire or kingdom, but the melting away of the lovers' power over their realms.

O Romeo, Romeo, Wherefore Art Thou Romeo?

JULIET: O Romeo, Romeo, wherefore art thou Romeo?
Deny thy father and refuse thy name;
Or if thou wilt not, be but sworn my love
And I'll no longer be a Capulet.

ROMEO: [*Aside*] Shall I hear more, or shall I speak at this?
JULIET: 'Tis but thy name that is my enemy:
      Thou art thyself, though not a Montague.
      What's Montague? It is nor hand nor foot,
      Nor arm nor face, nor any other part
      Belonging to a man. O be some other name!
      What's in a name? That which we call a rose
      By any other word would smell as sweet;
      So Romeo would, were he not Romeo call'd,
      Retain that dear perfection which he owes
      Without that title. Romeo, doff thy name,
      and for thy name, which is no part of thee,
      Take all myself.

ROMEO AND JULIET   **Act 2, scene 2, 33–49**

In the most famous scene of the play, Romeo stands unnoticed beneath Juliet's balcony as she engages in a fantasized debate. She questions the purpose of Romeo's being Romeo—something he's probably taken for granted all these years. That Romeo is Romeo creates a few rather touchy problems for the new lovebirds. To be Romeo is to be a Montague while to be Juliet is to be a Capulet, and the Montagues and Capulets have a nasty history of killing off one another. Juliet fancies that family identity can be changed along with one's name, and family fueds thus nullified.

O ROMEO, ROMEO, WHEREFORE ART THOU ROMEO?

Although we use "wherefore," if at all, as a synonym for "why," Juliet uses the word in a more limited sense. By "wherefore?" Juliet means "for what purpose?" If she had merely asked "Why art thou Romeo?" she wouldn't be distinguishing the two major meanings of "why"—"from what cause" (in the past) and "for what purpose" (in the future). "Wherefore" clearly emphasizes the latter sense, which is why "whys and wherefores" are different things.

"Wherefore" and its partner "therefore" reflect the basic tendency of English to use spatial ideas—"where?" "there"— to represent logical ideas, such as cause and effect.

WHAT'S IN A NAME? THAT WHICH WE CALL A ROSE BY ANY OTHER WORD WOULD SMELL AS SWEET

If there's such a thing as generic Shakespeare today, this is it. Both "What's in a name?" and "A rose by any other name would smell as sweet" are Instant Bard, although the latter is, as many forget, merely a paraphrase. From the romantic declamation to the crass advertisement, these phrases have served generations with complete flexibility.

"What's in a name?" is the less specific of the two phrases, and also the less common. Juliet here merely rehearses in a different form the point of "What's a Montague," moving, like a good Renaissance student, from the particular to the general. Names in general, she insists, ought to be separable from the things they name. Romeo never does change his name, and it wouldn't have done much good anyway. Whether or not he's essentially a Montague, and Juliet essentially a Capulet, their families will continue to act that way.

"That which we call a rose/ By any other word would smell as sweet" seems bloated to the modern ear. But we're accustomed to the paraphrase, which never occurred to the playwright or his audience. It's a little futile to second-guess Shakespeare now, but he did have to fill out a line and a half of blank verse. Regarding Juliet's use of "word" instead of "name," we can perhaps be grateful; she already uses "name" six times in fifteen and a half lines.

A Round Unvarnished Tale

OTHELLO: Yet (by your gracious patience)
I will a round unvarnish'd tale deliver
Of my whole course of love—what drugs, what charms,
What conjuration, and what mighty magic
(For such proceeding I am charg'd withal)
I won his daughter.

OTHELLO **Act 1, scene 3, 89–94**

When Brabantio, a Venetian senator, discovers that his daughter Desdemona has eloped with the Moor Othello, he is stunned. The only way he can comprehend the event is to imagine Othello's employing all sorts of drugs and black magic on his normally timid daughter. In front of the Duke of Venice and the Senate, Othello steps forward to defend himself with "a round unvarnish'd tale." Here "round" means "straightforward" and "plain"; when an Elizabethan said that he would be "round with you," he meant that he would speak frankly. Othello disavows rhetorical tricks: his tale will be "unvarnish'd," eschewing any beguiling adornments or misleading artifice.

Yet Othello is not quite true to his word; to use both "round" and "unvarnish'd"—which are here nearly synonymous—is already to engage in artful speech. And by at first repeating the charges against him, almost as if to admit to them, he generates suspense and rhetorically misleads the audience. Othello repeatedly claims that he is "rude" in his speech, but nevertheless always speaks artfully. In this, he is like Marc Antony in *Julius Caesar* [see FRIENDS, ROMANS, COUNTRYMEN LEND ME YOUR EARS], or *Hamlet's* Polonius, Shakespeare's parody of the artfully artless rhetorician [see MORE MATTER WITH LESS ART].

Salad Days

CHARMIAN: O that brave Caesar!
CLEOPATRA: Be chok'd with such another emphasis!
                  Say "the brave Antony."
CHARMIAN: The valiant Caesar!
CLEOPATRA: By Isis, I will give thee bloody teeth,
                  If thou with Caesar paragon again
                  My man of men.

CHARMIAN: By your most gracious pardon,
            I sing but after you.
CLEOPATRA: My salad days,
            When I was green in judgment, cold in blood,
            To say as I said then!

ANTONY AND CLEOPATRA   Act 1, scene 5, 67–75

"Salad days" has probably generated as much confusion as any phrase in this book, excepting perhaps "hoist with his own petard." Some believe that "salad" refers to the sort of meal one was once, in less lavish (or more diet-conscious) days, forced to subsist on. Others think of their salad days as times of youthful innocence and indulgence, of brightly colored, freshly grown adventures. But the inventor of the phrase had neither romantic poverty nor flaming youth in mind.

By "salad days" Cleopatra refers to a time not when she had to *eat* salad, but when she was *like* salad. From the fifteenth century on, "salad" could mean any raw vegetable; metaphorically, the young Cleopatra was as "green" (inexperienced) and "cold" (passionless) as a piece of lettuce. At least, this is how she now explains her youthful affair with Julius Caesar.

The queen's attendant Charmian mocks her gushing tributes to her current lover, Marc Antony, comparing them to her past praises of the "valiant Caesar." Cleopatra, now middle-aged, snorts at the comparison. Her affair with Caesar, she insists, was never real, and her words then were meaningless. Her "judgment" (discretion, taste) and "blood" (passion) have matured; she portrays her "salad days" as a time of unreflective indulgence.

Screw Your Courage to the Sticking Place

MACBETH: If we should fail?

LADY MACBETH: We fail?
        But screw your courage to the sticking place,
        And we'll not fail.

MACBETH   Act 1, scene 7, 59–61

This is one time when you don't have to feel ignorant because you don't understand what Shakespeare really meant. Although he invented "sticking place," and though our usage derives directly from this scene, Shakespeare never explains what the phrase means.

Macbeth still has cold feet; he and his wife have agreed to kill King Duncan of Scotland, but he can't stop thinking of all the consequences the deed might not trammel up [*see* THE BE-ALL AND THE END-ALL]. Lady Macbeth, after impugning her husband's manliness, urges him, as we might say, to "screw up his courage." The *OED* suggests that Lady Macbeth's original words refer to the twisting of a tuning peg until it becomes set in its hole. The editor of *The Riverside Shakespeare*, on the other hand, suggests that a "sticking place" is "the mark to which a soldier screwed up the cord of a crossbow." Whether the metaphor is musical, martial, or otherwise, Lady Macbeth's meaning is obvious though her words are obscure: "tighten up your courage until it is fixed in the place necessary for the murder of Duncan."

The Serpent's Egg

BRUTUS: And since the quarrel
             Will bear no color for the thing he is,
             Fashion it thus: that what he is, augmented,
             Would run to these and these extremities;
             And therefore think him as a serpent's egg,
             Which, hatch'd, would as his kind grow mischievous,
             And kill him in the shell.

JULIUS CAESAR   Act 2, scene 1, 28–34

Brutus, soliloquizing, casts about for a rationale to join the conspiracy to assassinate Caesar [*see* MASTERS OF THEIR FATES]. The problem is that, so far, Caesar has not taken much advantage of his new power. "The thing he is"—a reasonable, stable leader—lends no "color," or credibility, to the argument that he is a danger to Roman liberties.

In a passage remarkable for its feeling of spontaneous thought, Brutus proceeds by extrapolation. Take what Caesar is now, he argues, augment it, and the result looks more threatening. Caesar is a "serpent's egg," a tyrant waiting to be hatched. If we find the egg, we recognize the "kind" (species);

when the kind is dangerous, better to kill the creature in the shell than let it hatch to perform its mischief. The equivalent idiom today is "let's nip this problem in the bud."

Shall I Compare Thee to a Summer's Day?

> Shall I compare thee to a summer's day?
> Thou art more lovely and more temperate:
> Rough winds do shake the darling buds of May,
> And summer's lease hath all too short a date. . . .
>
> "Sonnet 18," 1–4

The speaker of this poem compares the best of days to a paragon of youth; and the paragon, probably a young nobleman, wins the competition. The speaker finds him lovelier and more "temperate" (mild) than the often punishing days of summer. (The poet changes his mind about this in later sonnets.) And while summer and its beauties pass away—its "lease" (tenure) has too short a "date" (duration)—the young man's good looks will endure: "thy eternal summer shall not fade" (line 9). But this isn't because the youth has lots of Retin-A stored away. His beauty will endure forever because this sonnet will endure forever [compare GILDED MONUMENTS].

We treat "Shall I compare thee to a summer's day" as a compliment to the lover whose glories are supposed to match summer's. The poet's point is different: the lover isn't measured against summer, summer is measured against the lover (as he's captured in poetry) and is found lacking.

How Sharper than a Serpent's Tooth

LEAR: If she must teem,
Create her child of spleen, that it may live
And be a thwart disnatur'd torment to her!
Let it stamp wrinkles in her brow of youth,
With cadent tears fret channels in her cheeks,
Turn all her mother's pains and benefits
To laughter and contempt, that she may feel
How sharper than a serpent's tooth it is
To have a thankless child!

KING LEAR Act 1, scene 4, 281–289

King Lear has cut a deal with the two more flattering of his
three daughters: he will turn power over to them as long as he
can keep the name and respect due to a king, and so long as
they alternately host him and his train of a hundred knights.
Once they've got the power, of course, Regan and Goneril
renege on their part of the bargain. When Goneril, as prelude
to disbanding Lear's miniature army, objects to the group's
rowdiness, the king is furious. Her ingratitude is to Lear
"sharper than a serpent's tooth." He demands that Nature
render Goneril infertile, or, if his daughter must "teem" (give
birth, like an animal), that her child be a "thwart disnatur'd
(unnatural and perverse) torment to her, as she is to him. He
vividly imagines a monstrous infant stamping wrinkles in Goneril's brow, and burning her cheeks with its "cadent" (falling)
tears.

Later, Lear complains to Regan—who will turn out to be, if
anything, worse than Goneril—of Goneril's "Sharp-tooth'd
unkindness" and her "serpent-like" tongue (Act 2, scene 4).
His snakelike daughters represent the bestiality of all women:
"Down from the waist they are Centaurs . . . Beneath is all
the fiends' " (Act 4, scene 6). As he plunges from indignation

into madness, Lear becomes more and more horrified at the act of generation, and of his spawning such monstrous children; but he deflects self-criticism into vilification of women.

Short Shrift

RATCLIFFE: Come, come, dispatch: the Duke would be at dinner;
Make a short shrift: he longs to see your head.
HASTINGS: O momentary grace of mortal men,
Which we more hunt for than the grace of God!

RICHARD THE THIRD Act 3, scene 4, 94–97

"Short shrift" is a darned confusing idiom. Some use "short shrift" as the equivalent of "quick work," while others seem to mean "inadequate time." Both meanings indirectly stem from Shakespeare's. "Shrift" means "confession," from the verb "shrive"—a priest "shrives" someone by hearing confession and allotting a penance. (From "shrive" we also derive "Shrove Tuesday," or Mardi Gras, the day of merriment before Ash Wednesday confession and the beginning of Lent.)

To "make a short shrift," then, literally means to make a brief confession. We use the phrase very differently today: short shrift is now something you are "given" rather than something you "make" or perform. And to "give short shrift" is simply to allot small consideration to a person or idea; the notions of contrition and penance, once the essence of the phrase's irony, are now given short shrift.

As the bloody War of the Roses enters its final phase, Richard Duke of Gloucester rounds up everyone he deems an enemy, including his former accomplice Hastings. According to Richard's henchman Ratcliffe, Hastings's execution is holding up Richard's dinner. He advises the doomed Hastings to repent his sins as quickly as possible—to "make a short shrift" —so that his execution may proceed apace. Hastings suddenly realizes that Richard's courtesies to him were all manipulations, and that his own efforts to seek the grace of powerful men like Edward IV and Richard were doomed to fail. The grace of men is a sometime thing, determined by self-interest; only the grace of God endures.

Sigh No More, *Ladies,* *Sigh* No More

BALTHASAR: Sigh no more, ladies, sigh no more,
      Men were deceivers ever,
    One foot in sea, and one on shore,
      To one thing constant never.
    Then sigh not so, but let them go,
      And be you blithe and bonny,
    Converting all your sounds of woe
      Into hey nonny nonny.

MUCH ADO ABOUT NOTHING　Act 2, scene 3, 62–69

At the request of the prince, Don Pedro, his attendant Balthasar sings this little tune in their host's garden. The point of the ditty—that because men will never change their ways, women should just merrily accept them as they are—is clear enough, but its relevance to the play isn't. But at least one male character, and as many as three, will come to the conclusion that women (including the chaste heroine Hero) were deceivers ever, and raise no little fuss about it. Their sounds of woe become sounds of rage, rather than "hey nonny nonny" ("what the heck").

It Smells to Heaven

KING: O, my offense is rank, it smells to heaven,
   It hath the primal eldest curse upon't—
   A brother's murther. Pray can I not,
   Though inclination be as sharp as will.

HAMLET   Act 3, scene 3, 36–39

The fear of God has been put into King Claudius by a little drama piece Hamlet produced at court. As Hamlet had hoped, the play—which recreated Claudius's fratricide—caught Claudius's conscience [*see* THE PLAY'S THE THING]. In this soliloquy, Claudius confesses the deed and recoils at its smell. It is "rank" (that is, "rancid"), so rank that the vile odor wafts all the way to heaven. Thoughts of heaven remind him that his crime is the same as Cain's, a crime marked by the "primal eldest curse." Unfortunately for Claudius, although his inclination to repent is as "sharp as will" (is as keen as a desire), he's unable to pray for forgiveness, because he's unwilling to forfeit his ungodly gains.

So while Claudius is metaphorical about the "smell" of his deed, he is grimly literal about heaven's reaction. We, on the other hand, treat heaven as part of the metaphor. "It smells to heaven" has become pure hyperbole, a grander version of "it stinks."

So Sweet Was Never So Fatal

OTHELLO: One more, one more.
   Be thus when thou art dead, and I will kill thee
   And love thee after. One more, and that's the last.
   So sweet was ne'er so fatal. I must weep,

But they are cruel tears. This sorrow's heavenly,
It strikes where it doth love.

OTHELLO   Act 5, scene 2, 17–22

In this gruesome scene, Othello smothers his wife with kisses as he prepares to smother her—for real—in her sleep. Though he imagines himself as an agent of heaven, he still has trouble bringing himself to avenge his wife's supposed adulteries. As it turns out, Othello has been massively deluded by the scheming Iago, who has built up a circumstantial case against the chaste Desdemona, a case the guileless and sexually anxious Moor has all too willingly swallowed.

What Othello means by "So sweet was never so fatal" is not entirely clear. Perhaps he thinks that Desdemona's very sweetness has brought about her own destruction, because it has led her into amatory affairs. Or perhaps he refers to his own kisses, full of tenderness yet at the same time a prelude to murder. In either case, a living Desdemona is too "sweet" for Othello to handle. He would prefer a motionless, statuelike Desdemona —fixed, passive, completely in his possession.

Something Is Rotten in the State of Denmark

HORATIO: He waxes desperate with imagination.
MARCELLUS: Let's follow. 'Tis not fit thus to obey him.
HORATIO: Have after. To what issue will this come?
MARCELLUS: Something is rotten in the state of Denmark.
HORATIO: Heaven will direct it.
MARCELLUS: Nay, let's follow him. [*Exeunt.*]

HAMLET   Act 1, scene 4, 87–91

This is one time when the popular misquotation—"Something's rotten in Denmark"—is a real improvement on the original. But you ought to be careful around purists, who will also remember that the minor character Marcellus, and not Hamlet, is the one who coins the phrase. There's a reason he says "state of Denmark" rather than just Denmark: the fish is rotting from the head down—all is not well at the top of the political hierarchy.

There have been some hair-raising goings-on outside the castle at Elsinore. As the terrified Horatio and Marcellus look on, the ghost of the recently deceased king appears to Prince Hamlet. The spirit beckons Hamlet offstage, and the frenzied prince follows after, ordering the witnesses to stay put. They quickly decide to tag along anyway—it's not "fit" to obey someone who is in such a desperate state. In this confused exchange, Marcellus's famous non sequitur sustains the foreboding mood of the disjointed and mysterious action. And it reinforces the point and tone of some of Hamlet's earlier remarks—for example, that Denmark is "an unweeded garden" of "things rank and gross in nature" (Act 1, scene 2). When his father's ghost tells him his chilling tale in scene 5, the prince will realize just how rotten things *really* are in Denmark.

Something Wicked This Way Comes

2ND WITCH: By the pricking of my thumbs,
        Something wicked this way comes. [*Knocking*]
           Open locks,
           Whoever knocks!
           [*Enter Macbeth*]

MACBETH: How now, you secret, black, and midnight hags!
What is't you do?

MACBETH Act 4, scene 1, 44–49

After conjuring up "double, double toil and trouble" [*see* p. 32], the three witches admit a visitor to their cave—King Macbeth of Scotland. "Something wicked this way comes," indeed, and they're delighted. Macbeth—at least, the wicked Macbeth—is in part their own creation. The first time around, *they* came looking for *him*, to deliver the enticing prophecy that set off the whole chain of events which has included Macbeth's regicide and subsequent bloody events. Now, Macbeth comes looking for *them*, and the witches summon apparitions to tell Macbeth exactly what he wants to hear: that he's invulnerable. This news is purposely ambiguous; it is calculated only to make Macbeth act more wickedly before he is finally finished off.

A Sorry Sight

MACBETH: [Looking on his hands] This is a sorry sight.
LADY MACBETH: A foolish thought, to say a sorry sight.
MACBETH: There's one did laugh in 's sleep, and one cried,
        "Murther!"
    That they did wake each other. I stood and heard
        them;
    But they did say their prayers, and address'd them
    Again to sleep.

MACBETH Act 2, scene 2, 18–23

Macbeth's hands are a "sorry sight"—they're covered with the blood of King Duncan, whom he has just murdered. Macbeth seems to fuse several related meanings of "sorry." On one hand, the sight is "painful" or "distressing"; on the other, it provokes remorse and sorrow. We use "sorry sight" in a somewhat weaker sense than Macbeth did; we mean "pathetic spectacle." Serious pain or true regret is rarely involved.

Lady Macbeth only finds it foolish to get all emotional about such a manly deed of courage [see SCREW YOUR COURAGE TO THE STICKING PLACE]. Macbeth's bad conscience, however, cannot be curbed, as he hallucinates hideous denunciations of the murder.

There Is Special Providence in the Fall of a Sparrow

HORATIO: If your mind dislike any thing, obey it. I will forestall their repair hither, and say you are not fit.
HAMLET: Not a whit, we defy augury. There is special providence in the fall of a sparrow. If it be now, 'tis not to come; if it be not to

come, it will be now; if it be not now, yet it will come—the
readiness is all. Since no man, of aught he leaves, knows what is't
to leave betimes, let be.

HAMLET Act 5, scene 2, 217–224

Hamlet's stepfather, King Claudius, has arranged a fencing
match between the prince and Laertes. Laertes happens to be
the son of Polonius (whom Hamlet has slain) and the brother
of Ophelia (who has gone mad and committed suicide as a
result of Hamlet's actions). Hamlet and his friend Horatio well
know that the king desperately wants the prince out of the
way, and that Laertes is looking for revenge; the fencing match
doesn't promise to be an entirely playful affair.

Hamlet has agreed to it nonetheless, and refuses Horatio's
offer to excuse him if he thinks better of things. "We defy
augury"—that is, omens mean nothing to him. Hamlet will
deliver himself over to his fate, because he finally realizes that
it is out of his control. Before, he would have thought too
precisely on the event, weighed its implications, and sought
into its causes. Now, he is of the opinion that "there's special
providence in the fall of a sparrow," and therefore a guiding
hand behind his own fall, whenever it comes, now or in the
future. Here, Hamlet echoes the Gospel according to St. Mat-
thew, chapter 10: "And fear not them which kill the body, but
are not able to kill the soul: but rather fear him which is able
to destroy both soul and body in hell./ Are not two sparrows
sold for a farthing? and one of them shall not fall on the ground
without your Father" (King James version).

A Spotless Reputation

MOWBRAY: My dear dear lord,
    The purest treasure mortal times afford
    Is spotless reputation—that away,
    Men are but gilded loam, or painted clay.
    A jewel in a ten-times barr'd-up chest
    Is a bold spirit in a loyal breast.

           RICHARD THE SECOND Act 1, scene 1, 176–181

"Reputation" in the sense of one's good name dates only from the mid-sixteenth century, and "spotless reputation" seems to originate here. Thomas Mowbray, Duke of Norfolk, is in a high passion because Henry Bullingbrook, the future Henry IV, has accused him of treason, and the mere accusation sullies his reputation. King Richard calls for moderation and patience, but Mowbray demurs with this much-admired speech, which sums up one line of contemporary thought on the worth and dignity of Man. Without good name, Mowbray insists, a man is merely "gilded loam or painted clay," what Beatrice would call in *Much Ado about Nothing* "valiant dust" [*see* p. 168]. Without public honor, a man's inner virtues are like a jewel locked with ten bolts in an obscure chest. In the Renaissance, denigrating a man's name was occasion for a duel, and a duel soon ensues after Mowbray's fine speech. His sentiments are echoed both sincerely and parodically many times over in Shakespeare, for example by Iago [*see* WHO STEALS MY PURSE STEALS TRASH].

Who Steals My Purse Steals Trash

IAGO: Good name in man and woman, dear my lord,
    Is the immediate jewel of their souls.
    Who steals my purse steals trash; 'tis something, nothing;
    'Twas mine, 'tis his, and has been slave to thousands;
    But he that filches from me my good name
    Robs me of that which not enriches him,
    And makes me poor indeed.

                       OTHELLO Act 3, scene 3, 155–161

At this point in *Othello,* our hero has just begun his precipitous fall into Iago's intricate trap. Iago hints that one of Othello's officers, Cassio, has been making time with Othello's wife. On top of this innuendo he plasters a seeming reluctance to reveal the fictitious affair, because that would ruin Cassio's reputation —and to "filch" from someone his good name is a much more serious crime than stealing his purse. Honor is an essential possession, something that can belong to you and to you only; your money, on the other hand, remains what it is even if thousands of others have handled and possessed it. Compared to honor, then, money is mere "trash."

Iago's speech is in ironic contrast to his exhortations of Roderigo to "put money in thy purse [see p. 118]. When it suits his purposes better, Iago can exclaim that virtue's "a fig" (Act 1, scene 3, 319), and that reputation is merely something one cultivates in order to hide his true intentions. It rather suits his purposes here, however, to cloak his evil intentions—his desire to ruin Othello's marriage—in the pieties of friendship and sacred respect for another man's honor.

Sterner Stuff

MARCUS ANTONIUS: When that the poor have cried, Caesar hath wept;
　　　　　　　　Ambition should be made of sterner stuff:
　　　　　　　　Yet Brutus says he was ambitious,
　　　　　　　　And Brutus is an honorable man.

　　　　　　　　　　　　　　　　　JULIUS CAESAR　Act 3, scene 2, 91–94

Marc Antony continues, with bitter irony, to manipulate his friends, Romans, and countrymen [see p. 44]. This is his funeral oration for the murdered Julius Caesar, and he's speaking with the permission of the honorable Brutus, one of the assassins. Brutus had earlier questioned the crowd, rhetorically, whether they had "rather Caesar were living, and die all slaves, than that Caesar were dead, to live all freemen" (lines 22–24). Antony mocks the notion that Caesar had ambitions to rule over his jealously republican countrymen. He paints Caesar as a tenderhearted friend of the poor, just as he will paint Brutus as a coldhearted traitor to his friend Caesar [see THE MOST UNKINDEST CUT OF ALL].

We use "sterner stuff" primarily to mean "sturdier stuff"; Antony implies as much, but his literal sense ("sterner" meaning "harsher") is more appropriate. Antony's intention is to embellish Caesar's kindheartedness, almost to the point of calling him weak. Caesar comes off a helpless victim; Brutus and company loom as stern assassins. Given the danger he faces while the conspirators are effectively in control of the state, Antony cloaks his point in irony, but only thinly. He repeats "Brutus is an honorable man" four times in seventeen lines, leaving no one in doubt as to his true meaning.

Strange Bedfellows

TRINCULO: Legg'd like a man! and his fins like arms! Warm, o' my troth! I do now let loose my opinion, hold it no longer: this is no fish, but an islander, that hath lately suffer'd by a thunder-bolt. [*Thunder.*] Alas, the storm is come again! My best way is to creep under his gaberdine; there is no other shelter hereabout: misery acquaints a man with strange bedfellows. I will here shroud till the dregs of the storm be past.

THE TEMPEST Act 2, scene 2, 33–41

A storm has shipwrecked Trinculo, a jester, with his aristocratic keepers on an uncharted island. Trinculo happens upon the supine form of Caliban, a deformed native whom he first takes to be some sort of strange fish. When he realizes that Caliban has arms and legs and is warm-blooded, he correctly deduces that what seemed a fish is an islander.

As the storm resumes and thunder sounds, Trinculo is forced into the nearest shelter, which happens to be Caliban's gaberdine (a loose-fitting cloak). As Trinculo famously puts it, "misery acquaints a man with strange bedfellows," and he uses the phrase more literally than we do. He must, to avoid the storm, actually lie down with the petrified Caliban (who thinks Trinculo a tormenting spirit) and share his garment as bedclothing. Trinculo's "strange" can mean either "foreign," "unknown," or "odd," while we use "strange" only in the last sense. We've also adapted the phrase to more metaphorical uses, meaning by "strange bedfellows" unexpected partners.

Strive Mightily

HORTENSIO: Sir, you say well, and well you do conceive,
And since you do profess to be a suitor,
You must, as we do, gratify this gentleman,
To whom we all rest generally beholding.

TRANIO: Sir, I shall not be slack; in sign whereof,
Please ye we may contrive this afternoon,
And quaff carouses to our mistress' health,
And do as adversaries do in law,
Strive mightily, but eat and drink as friends.

THE TAMING OF THE SHREW Act 1, scene 2, 269–277

Today, one "strives mightily" against great odds to secure some noble, usually unselfish, end. In *The Taming of the Shrew*, however, Tranio doesn't have heroic deeds in mind. The situation he likens to a law case is a three-way competition for the hand of the beautiful and well-dowered Bianca; the suitors are compared to opposed lawyers with only a professional interest in the competition. Nothing so important or so personal is at stake that the opponents can't share a nip at the metaphorical men's club.

Tranio is actually a sham, a decoy for his master Lucentio, who *is* a suitor. Tranio and Lucentio have exchanged roles so that Lucentio, in the guise of a tutor, can spend hours covertly courting his "pupil" Bianca. Tranio's job is to keep Bianca's other suitors and her father off Lucentio's scent. If all this sounds confusing, things get a lot more complicated before the inevitable happy ending.

Such Stuff as Dreams Are Made on

PROSPERO: Our revels now are ended. These our actors,
As I foretold you, were all spirits, and
Are melted into air, into thin air:
And like the baseless fabric of this vision,
The cloud-capp'd tow'rs, the gorgeous palaces,
The solemn temples, the great globe itself,
Yea, all which it inherit, shall dissolve,
And, like this insubstantial pageant faded,
Leave not a rack behind. We are such stuff
As dreams are made on; and our little life
Is rounded with a sleep.

THE TEMPEST   Act 4, scene 1, 148–158

Anticipating his daughter's wedding to the Prince of Naples, Prospero has staged a short entertainment, with spirits taking the parts of Roman gods. But he abruptly cuts the fun short when he remembers some pressing business. He tries to calm the startled couple by explaining, somewhat off the point, that the "revels" (performance) they've witnessed were simply an illusion, bound sooner or later to melt into "thin air"—a phrase he coins.

Prospero's metaphor applies not just to the pageant he's created on his fictional island, but also to the pageant Shakespeare presents in his Globe Theater—the "great globe itself." Dramatic illusion in turn becomes a metaphor for the "real" world outside the Globe, which is equally fleeting. Towers, palaces, temples, the Globe theater, the Earth—all will crumble and dissolve, leaving not even a wisp of cloud (a "rack") behind. Prospero's "pageant" is the innermost Chinese box: a play within a play (*The Tempest*) within a play (the so-called "real" world).

Merrily, merrily, merrily, merrily, life is but a dream, and people are the "stuff" dreams are "made on" (built of)—just as characters might be called the "stuff" plays are "built on." "Our little life" is like a brief dream in some divine mind, "rounded with a sleep"—that is, either "surrounded" by sleep or "rounded off" (completed) by sleep. Prospero seems to mean that when we die, we awake from the dream of life into true reality—or at least into a truer dream.

"The stuff of dreams" seems to derive from this passage, but it only superficially resembles Prospero's pronouncement. "The stuff of dreams" as we use it today refers to a scenario one can only fantasize—something devoutly to be wished. Prospero's "stuff" refers to the materials that go into creating an illusion, not to the object of a wish.

Take note that Prospero says "made on," not "made of," despite Humphrey Bogart's famous last line in the 1941 film *The Maltese Falcon:* "The stuff that dreams are made of." (Bogart suggested the line to director John Huston, but neither seems to have brushed up his Shakespeare.) Film buffs may think "made of" is the authentic phrase, but they're only dreaming.

Sweet Are the Uses of Adversity

DUKE SENIOR: Sweet are the uses of adversity,
                Which, like the toad, ugly and venomous,
                Wears yet a precious jewel in his head;
                And this our life, exempt from public haunt,
                Finds tongues in trees, books in the running brooks,
                Sermons in stones, and good in every thing.

                                    AS YOU LIKE IT Act 2, scene 1, 12–17

The duke is describing the world view he's been forced to adopt now that he's been deposed and exiled by his villainous brother —this is the "adversity" for which he has found "sweet uses." By "uses," the duke means "profits." He compares his seeming suffering—for example, exposure to the elements—to an ugly toad, which legendarily had a "precious jewel" with healing qualities embedded in its temple. The jewel he discovers in his condition—its profit—is freedom from "public haunt," or society. The duke concludes that nature "speaks" more eloquently and truly than tongues, books, and sermons; stones turn out to be better company than courtiers.

The duke's metaphor now seems far-fetched, as it may also have seemed to Shakespeare's audience. Nevertheless, "sweet are the uses of adversity" survives as somewhat preciously sincere words of comfort, when not uttered sarcastically.

Sweets to the Sweet

HAMLET: What, the fair Ophelia!
QUEEN: [*Scattering flowers*] Sweets to the sweet, farewell!
          I hop'd thou shouldst have been my Hamlet's wife:
          I thought thy bride-bed to have deck'd, sweet maid,
          And not have strew'd thy grave.

HAMLET Act 5, scene 1, 242–246

When Hamlet's mother, the queen, delivers "Sweets to the sweet," she's not bearing a hostess gift or offering candy to her date. The queen's "sweets" are funeral bouquets scattered in the grave of Ophelia, Hamlet's former flame.

The prince, who has just finished addressing the skull of Yorick [*see* ALAS, POOR YORICK], stumbles upon the funeral, ignorant that Ophelia has likely committed suicide. The murder of her father had driven Ophelia mad; Hamlet was the murderer, and the queen a witness. This is all bad enough. But the queen's elegiac nostalgia for her son's courtship of this deceased "sweet" is all the more disturbing in light of Hamlet's somewhat over-arduous attachment to his mother.

It's therefore ironic that "sweets to the sweet" has become a corny quotation for those special romantic moments. How effective the line proves depends on how vividly one's "sweet" is likely to recall the graveyard scene in *Hamlet*. You might, however, find these bons mots most winning when offered with a willow branch and a whiff of charm to a soon-to-be-insignificant other.

Swift as a Shadow

LYSANDER: Or, if there were a sympathy in choice,
War, death, or sickness did lay siege to it,
Making it momentany as a sound,
Swift as a shadow, short as any dream,
Brief as the lightning in the collied night,
That, in a spleen, unfolds both heaven and earth;
And ere a man hath power to say "Behold!"
The jaws of darkness do devour it up:
So quick bright things come to confusion.

A MIDSUMMER NIGHT'S DREAM Act 1, scene 1, 141–149

Lysander is discoursing on true love, whose course, he has determined, "never did run smooth" [see p. 24]. Even granting that a courtship arises from "sympathy" (mutual desire) rather than family pressure, all kinds of difficulties will arise.

War, death, sickness—in short, the ravages of time—assail true lovers, making their passion as "momentany" (momentary) as a sound. ("Momentany" was a common form in the sixteenth and seventeenth centuries, although Shakespeare usually avoids it.)

Lysander gets caught up in this idea and generates more prolix metaphors for the brevity of love—it is as "swift" (fleeting) as a shadow, short as a dream on a midsummer night, brief as a flash of lightning. This flash "unfolds" (displays) heaven and earth in a brief burst, only to be swallowed up by the "jaws of darkness" that are the rest of human experience. ("Collied" means "as black as coal," deriving from the same root as "collier.") For Lysander, love is a "quick bright thing" brought to confusion by the inexorable workings of time and nature.

Lysander's "swift as a shadow," the most famous phrase from this speech, ultimately derives from the proverbial expression "to flee like a shadow," which dates from around the twelfth century.

Take Physic, Pomp

LEAR: Poor naked wretches, wheresoe'er you are,
That bide the pelting of this pitiless storm,
How shall your houseless heads and unfed sides,
Your loop'd and window'd raggedness, defend you
From seasons such as these? O, I have ta'en
Too little care of this! Take physic, pomp;
Expose thyself to feel what wretches feel,
That thou mayst shake the superflux to them,
And show the heavens more just.

KING LEAR   Act 3, scene 4, 28–36

King Lear's "Take physic, pomp" means "pompous men, take a taste of your own medicine." The medicine ("physic") he has in mind is a bitter concoction: exposure to such storms as Lear himself now endures, having been thrown out by his ungrateful daughters [see MORE SINNED AGAINST THAN SINNING]. For the first time in his royal life, Lear experiences what it's like to be a poor, naked wretch, and the feeling is unpleasant. The king realizes that his former comforts (his "pomp") prevented his administering compassionately to the wretches of his realm—he has taken "Too little care of this." Only a dose of human suffering can establish the difference between what is necessary in life and what is mere indulgence. Thus enlightened, the rich and pompous "mayst shake the superflux to them"—shake off what is superfluous and distribute it to the needy.

That Way Madness Lies

LEAR: No, I will weep no more. In such a night
       To shut me out? Pour on; I will endure.
       In such a night as this? O Regan, Goneril!
       Your old kind father, whose frank heart gave all—
       O, that way madness lies; let me shun that;
       No more of that.

                                    KING LEAR   Act 3, scene 4, 17–22

As the storm continues on the heath [see MORE SINNED AGAINST THAN SINNING], King Lear ponders filial ingratitude. His wicked daughters Regan and Goneril, between whom he divided his kingdom, have turned Lear out into a furious storm, just to show him who's really in charge. Since he has spent the last three scenes dwelling on his daughters' crimes, it's strange that Lear should now wish to sidestep the topic. "That way madness lies," he figures, and he's correct; he's been going mad for the length of Act 3, and it's another symptom of madness that he pretends to shun what he's already obsessed over.

Perhaps the king should ponder instead his own "frank heart." He seems to have dealt with his daughters—including the devoted and rejected Cordelia—more as a king than as a father. To recognize truly that he was "sinning" as well as "sinn'd against" would hasten his collapse.

That Within which Passes Show

QUEEN: Thou know'st 'tis common: all that lives must die,
            Passing through nature to eternity.
HAMLET: Ay, madam, it is common.
QUEEN: If it be,
            Why seems it so particular with thee?

HAMLET: Seems, madam? nay, it is, I know not "seems."
'Tis not alone my inky cloak, good mother,
Nor customary suits of solemn black,
Nor windy suspiration of forc'd breath,
No, nor the fruitful river in the eye,
Nor the dejected havior of the visage,
Together with all forms, moods, shapes of grief,
That can denote me truly. These indeed seem,
For they are actions that a man might play;
But I have that within which passes show,
These but the trappings and the suits of woe.

HAMLET   Act 1, scene 2, 72–86

The queen is peeved. Like her new husband Claudius, she upbraids her son for still mourning his father and for his conspicuous lack of enthusiasm for her recent marriage [see MORE THAN KIN AND LESS THAN KIND]. She finds Hamlet's mourning garb and heavy sighs a bit "particular"—everybody dies, so what's the big fuss? She insinuates that Hamlet is putting on a show just to get attention.

Hamlet snaps back with his famous repudiation of theatricality. His clothing and his gesture may "seem" to be a show; they are indeed things an actor could fabricate. But he has "that within which passes show," that is, feelings which *surpass* display. His tears, his sighs, his black clothes, his evident dejection are mere tokens of emotions that could never be fully expressed. But by dismissing the notion that he could act out his true self, Hamlet presents us with a paradox: how then could an audience ever understand him?

There Are More Things in Heaven and Earth, Horatio

HAMLET: Swear by my sword
           Never to speak of this that you have heard.
GHOST: [*Beneath*] Swear by his sword.
HAMLET: Well said, old mole, canst work i' th' earth so fast?
           A worthy pioner! Once more remove, good friends.
HORATIO: O day and night, but this is wondrous strange!
HAMLET: And therefore as a stranger give it welcome.
           There are more things in heaven and earth, Horatio,
           Than are dreamt of in your philosophy.

                                    HAMLET   Act 1, scene 5, 159–167

Horatio and Marcellus, though advised against it, barge into Hamlet's conversation with his father's ghost [see SOMETHING IS ROTTEN IN THE STATE OF DENMARK]. Hamlet is a little unforthcoming with the news imparted by this spirit, who is still rustling about under the stage. So it's hard to figure what Horatio and Marcellus are being asked to keep quiet, though Hamlet and the burrowing ghost (a "pioner," or miner) insist.

Horatio, a model of rationality, is still having a hard time swallowing the whole business. Ghosts are not the sort of beings his "philosophy" easily takes into account. We know that Horatio is, like Hamlet, a student at the University of Wittenberg, a notable outpost of Protestant humanism. The philosophy he studies there is probably classical—a compound of ethics, logic, and natural science. The emphasis on everyday phenomena pretty much excludes speculation about talking ghosts.

Wittenberg, however, isn't just a place where sober-minded Horatios debate Aristotelian physics. In Christopher Marlowe's play of the late 1580s, *Doctor Faustus*, it is where the doctor lectures and, on the sideline, fraternizes with demons.

This Thing of Darkness

PROSPERO: Mark but the badges of these men, my lords,
           Then say if they be true. This misshapen knave—
           His mother was a witch. . . .
           These three have robb'd me, and this demi-devil—
           For he's a bastard one—had plotted with them
           To take my life. Two of these fellows you
           Must know and own; this thing of darkness I
           Acknowledge mine.
CALIBAN: I shall be pinch'd to death.

THE TEMPEST   Act 5, scene 1, 267–276

The once and future Duke Prospero of Milan and his daughter are stranded on an island with the native "demi-devil" Caliban, the bastard son of a witch and a demon. Caliban is compelled into servitude, and Prospero keeps him in line by having the local spirits administer pinches when necessary.

In more recent days, Prospero and his spirits have shipwrecked his treacherous brother Antonio (now the duke) and other nemeses on the island. Toward the end of the play, after torturing *them* for four acts, he gives them a direct piece of his mind. In this scene, two drunks stumble in with Caliban, after Prospero has foiled their inept plot to seize the island. By their "badges" (emblems of their master), the men are identified as Antonio's lackeys, and Prospero dryly asks his brother whether his servants "be true" (are honest). But his contempt for them is more than matched by his disgust at his own rebellious slave, "this thing of darkness" which Prospero must "acknowledge mine."

Prospero's phrase recalls the way the clown Touchstone describes his rustic fiancée in the comedy *As You Like It:* "A poor virgin, sir, an ill-favor'd thing, sir, but mine own; a poor humor of mine, sir, to take that that no man else will" (Act 5, scene 4). Touchstone's "humanitarian" realism stands in marked contrast to Prospero's unforgiving vilification of the often sympathetic Caliban.

Thinking Too Precisely on the Event

HAMLET: Now whether it be
        Bestial oblivion, or some craven scruple
        Of thinking too precisely on th' event—
        A thought which, quarter'd, hath but one part wisdom
        And ever three parts coward—I do not know
        Why yet I live to say this thing's to do,
        Sith I have cause, and will, and strength, and means
        To do't.

                                        HAMLET Act 4, scene 4, 39–46

Having just encountered a Norwegian force on its way to contest "a little patch of ground" in Poland, the Prince of Denmark once again upbraids himself for being unable to act decisively. Commanded by his father's ghost to avenge his murder, Hamlet has as yet been unable to do the deed.

Hamlet's self-appraisals here echo earlier sentiments—that "conscience does make cowards of us all" and that "the native hue of resolution/ Is sicklied o'er with the pale cast of thought" [*see* TO BE, OR NOT TO BE, THAT IS THE QUESTION]. He spoke then of the fear of death; here, he speaks of "thinking" in general, the "precise" lingering over objections, reappraisals, calculations, implications, etc., to the point where action is stifled and opportunities missed. Hamlet—who may only *think* he's been thinking too much—thinks that thinking is only one part wise to three parts cowardly.

A Thousand Times Good Night

NURSE: [*Within*] Madam!
JULIET: I come, anon.—But if thou meanest not well,
　　　I do beseech thee—
NURSE: 　　　　Madam!
JULIET: 　　　　　　By and by, I come—
　　　To cease thy strife, and leave me to my grief.
　　　To-morrow will I send.
ROMEO: 　　　　So thrive my soul—
JULIET: A thousand times good night! [*Exit above*]
ROMEO: A thousand times the worse, to want thy light.
　　　Love goes toward love as schoolboys from their books,
　　　But love from love, toward school with heavy looks.

　　　　　　　　　ROMEO AND JULIET　Act 2, scene 2, 149–157

With her nurse on the lookout, Juliet wraps up, for now, her famous balcony conversation with Romeo [*see* O ROMEO, ROMEO, WHEREFORE ART THOU ROMEO?]. Punctuated by the nurse's warnings, Juliet's speech becomes distracted. Still un-sure of her feelings and of Romeo's love, she nervously pleads that if his intentions are merely to toy with her (if he means not well), he should just leave her alone. Then she turns around, pledges to send a message to him on the morrow, and parts with her famous "A thousand times good night!"

Romeo refers yet again to Juliet as a source of light [*see* WHAT LIGHT THROUGH YONDER WINDOW BREAKS?]. Then he delivers a revealing couplet that sounds like a scene-ender, but (as much as we might hope it is) is not. The young lovebird, if he's not still in school, isn't long out of it; so perhaps it's natural for him to compare Juliet to a schoolbook. But note the artful inversion: he "goes toward" his lover as he leaves school, eagerly, and leaves her as he goes to school, "with heavy looks." Other Shakespearean characters echo Romeo's antipathy for the classroom. In a later play, the satirist Jaques describes youth, the second age of man, with this image: "the whining schoolboy, with his satchel/ And shining morning face, creeping like a snail/ Unwillingly to school" (*As You Like It*, Act 2, scene 7, 145–147).

Thrift, Thrift, Horatio

HORATIO: My lord, I came to see your father's funeral.
HAMLET: I prithee do not mock me, fellow student,
    I think it was to see my mother's wedding.
HORATIO: Indeed, my lord, it followed hard upon.
HAMLET: Thrift, thrift, Horatio, the funeral bak'd-meats
    Did coldly furnish forth the marriage tables.

HAMLET   Act 1, scene 2, 176–181

Hamlet isn't the only one who has noticed how hastily his mother has remarried after her husband's death [*see* FRAILTY, THY NAME IS WOMAN]. Horatio, a fellow "student" (student) at the University of Wittenberg, agrees that the wedding followed "hard upon" the funeral. Hamlet's "Thrift, thrift, Horatio," adopted into modern English as a sort of recommendation, is actually an ironic condemnation. With the usual dose of black humor, he explains the hastiness of the marriage as an attempt to economize: the leftovers from the funeral (the "bak'd-meats") could be served cold at the wedding feast. What state these meats would be in after almost a month is left to our imagination.

There Is a Tide in the Affairs of Men

BRUTUS: There is a tide in the affairs of men
　　　　Which, taken at the flood, leads on to fortune;
　　　　Omitted, all the voyage of their life
　　　　Is bound in shallows and in miseries.
　　　　On such a full sea are we now afloat,
　　　　And we must take the current when it serves,
　　　　Or lose our ventures.

JULIUS CAESAR   **Act 4, scene 3, 218–224**

Brutus and Cassius are discussing the final phase of their civil war with the forces of Octavian and Marcus Antonius. Cassius

has been urging that they group their forces at Sardis and take advantage of the secure location to catch their breath. Brutus, however, advocates heading off the enemy at Philippi before Octavian can recruit more men. Brutus's main point is that, since "the enemy increaseth every day" and "We, at the height, are ready to decline" (lines 216–217), he and Cassius must act now while the ratio of forces is most advantageous. "There's a tide in the affairs of men," he insists; that is, power is a force that ebbs and flows in time, and one must "go with the flow." Waiting around only allows your power to pass its crest and begin to ebb; if the opportunity is "omitted" (missed), you'll find yourself stranded in miserable shallows.

The Time Is out of Joint

HAMLET: Let us go in together,
         And still your fingers on your lips, I pray.
         The time is out of joint—O cursèd spite,
         That ever I was born to set it right!
         Nay, come, let's go together.

                              HAMLET   Act 1, scene 5, 186–190

To Hamlet, the state of affairs (the "time") in Denmark resembles a dislocated shoulder, "out of joint." He sees himself as the physician who will have to operate on the crippled kingdom not just by setting the bones, but also by removing a cancer: King Claudius.

The dour Dane mutters these sentiments after encountering his father's ghost. We have seen that he is already plotting the way to "heal" the time—by first pretending to be sick himself [*see* ANTIC DISPOSITION]. But while he speaks to his companions with resolution, in these remarks which end the first act he betrays feelings of resentment and unfitness to the task. These feelings will become the subject of his greatest soliloquies.

To Be, or Not to Be

HAMLET: *To be, or not to be, that is the question:*
Whether 'tis nobler in the mind to suffer
The slings and arrows of outrageous fortune,
Or to take arms against a sea of troubles
And by opposing end them. To die—to sleep,
No more; and by a sleep to say we end
The heart-ache and the thousand natural shocks
That flesh is heir to: 'tis a consummation
Devoutly to be wish'd. To die, to sleep;
To sleep, perchance to dream—ay, *there's the rub:*
For in that sleep of death what dreams may come,
When we have shuffled off *this mortal coil,*

Must give us pause—there's the respect
That makes calamity of so long life.
For who would bear the whips and scorns of time,
Th'oppressor's wrong, the proud man's contumely,
The pangs of dispriz'd love, the law's delay,
The insolence of office, and the spurns
That patient merit of th'unworthy takes,
When he himself might *his quietus make*
With a bare bodkin? Who would fardels bear,
To grunt and sweat under a weary life,
But that the dread of something after death,
The undiscover'd country, from whose bourn
No traveller returns, puzzles the will,
And makes us rather bear those ills we have
Than fly to others that we know not of?
Thus conscience does make cowards of us all,
And thus the native hue of resolution
Is sicklied o'er with the pale cast of thought,
And enterprises of great pitch and moment
With this regard their currents turn awry
And lose the name of action.

HAMLET   Act 3, scene 1, 55–87 [Italics mine]

Probably the best-known lines in English literature, Hamlet's greatest soliloquy is the source of more than a dozen everyday (or everymonth) expressions—the stuff that newspaper editorials and florid speeches are made on. Rather than address every one of these gems, I've selected a few of the richer ones for comment. But rest assured that you can quote any line and people will recognize your erudition.

Hamlet, in contemplating the nature of action, characteristically waxes existential, and it is this quality—the sense that here we have Shakespeare's own ideas on the meaning of life and death—that has made the speech so quotable. Whether or not Shakespeare endorsed Hamlet's sentiments, he rose to the occasion with a very great speech on the very great topic of human "being."

The subtle twists and turns of the prince's language I shall leave to the critics. My focus will be on the isolated images Hamlet invokes, the forgotten pictures behind the words, the parts we ignore when we quote the sum.

TO BE, OR NOT TO BE, THAT IS THE QUESTION

If you follow Hamlet's speech carefully, you'll notice that his notions of "being" and "not being" are rather complex. He doesn't simply ask whether life or death is preferable; it's hard to clearly distinguish the two—"being" comes to look a lot like "not being," and vice versa. To be, in Hamlet's eyes, is a passive state, to "suffer" outrageous fortune's blows, while not being is the action of opposing those blows. Living is, in effect, a kind of slow death, a submission to fortune's power. On the other hand, death is initiated by a life of action, rushing armed against a sea of troubles—a pretty hopeless project, if you think about it.

TO SLEEP, PERCHANCE TO DREAM

Hamlet tries to take comfort in the idea that death is really "no more" than a kind of sleep, with the advantage of one's never having to get up in the morning. This is a "consummation"—a completion or perfection—"devoutly to be wish'd," or piously prayed for. What disturbs Hamlet, however, is that if death is a kind of sleep, then it might entail its own dreams, which would become a new life—these dreams are the hereafter, and the hereafter is a frightening unknown. Hamlet's hesitation is akin to that of the condemned hero Claudio in *Measure for Measure*, written a few years after *Hamlet*. "Ay, but to die," he considers, "and go we know not where;/ To lie in cold obstruction, and to rot . . ." (Act 3, scene 1). Hamlet's fear is less clearly visualized, but is of the same type. No matter how miserable life is, both heroes suppose, people prefer it to death because there's always a chance that the life after death will be worse.

THERE'S THE RUB

We say "there's the rub" and think we communicate perfectly well—but do we? I mean "there's the catch" while you might think "there's the essence"—the meanings can be close, yet they're not identical. Shakespeare implies both senses, but calls up a concrete picture which would have been familiar to his audience. "Rub" is the sportsman's name for an obstacle which, in the game of bowls, diverts a ball from its true course. The Bard was obviously fond of the sport (he played on lawns, not lanes): he uses bowling analogies frequently and expertly. This is the most famous of such analogies, though not as elaborate as "Like to a bowl upon a subtle ground,/ I have tumbled past the throw" (*Coriolanus*, Act 5, scene 2). Although "rub" is used figuratively here, the image that leaps to Hamlet's mind is vivid and homely. Hamlet is often homely at odd moments, especially when the topic is death. "I'll lug the guts into the neighbor room" is another good example.

THIS MORTAL COIL

Shakespeare is really twisting syntax with this one. "Coil" generally means a "fuss" or a "to-do"—as in the line, "for the wedding being here to-morrow, there is a great coil tonight" (*Much Ado about Nothing*, Act 3, scene 3). But a to-do can't be "mortal," so what Hamlet must mean is "this tumultuous world of mortals."

This phrase succinctly illustrates the power Shakespeare can achieve by employing words with radically different origins and uses. "Quietus" is Latinate and legalistic; "bodkin" is concrete and probably Celtic in origin. Here, "his quietus make" means something like "even the balance" or "settle his accounts for good." That he might do this with a "bodkin"—elsewhere in Shakespeare a kind of knitting-needle, here a dagger—puts more menace in the abstract, almost clinical "quietus." "Fardels," "grunt," and "sweat" pick up on the grunting and sweating sound of "bodkin." "Fardel," a pack or bundle, is derived from the Arabic *fardah* (package): "grunt" and "sweat" are rooted in good old Anglo-Saxon. Hamlet's "fardels" are the wearying burdens of a weary life.

THE UNDISCOVERED COUNTRY, FROM WHOSE BOURN NO TRAVELLER RETURNS

Comfortably back in the high diction appropriate to a noble soliloquizer, Hamlet pulls out all the stops. He may be likening the unimaginable "something after death" to the New World, from which, in this Age of Exploration, some travelers were returning and some weren't. "Bourn" literally means "limit" or "boundary"; to cross the border into the country of death, he says, is an irreversible act. But Hamlet forgets that he has had a personal conversation with one traveler who *has* returned—his father, whose ghost has disclosed the details of his own murder [*see* THERE ARE MORE THINGS IN HEAVEN AND EARTH, HORATIO].

THUS CONSCIENCE DOES MAKE COWARDS OF US ALL

Hamlet's phrase is certainly the most famous judgment on fear of the unknown. But he was not the first of Shakespeare's characters to utter such words: King Richard III, on the verge of his downfall, had said that "Conscience is but a word that cowards use,/ Devis'd at first to keep the strong in awe" (*Richard III*, Act 5, scene 3). The difference is that Machiavellian Richard professes not to believe in (or even have) a conscience, though his bad dreams ought to have convinced him otherwise. Hamlet believes in conscience; he just questions whether it's always appropriate [see THINKING TOO PRECISELY ON THE EVENT].

To Thine Own Self Be True

POLONIUS: This above all: to thine own self be true,
And it must follow, as the night the day,
Thou canst not then be false to any man.
Farewell, my blessing season this in thee!

LAERTES: Most humbly do I take my leave, my lord.

HAMLET Act 1, scene 3, 78–82

"To thine own self be true" is Polonius's last piece of advice to his son Laertes, who is in a hurry to get on the next boat to Paris, where he'll be safe from his father's long-winded speeches [see NEITHER A BORROWER NOR A LENDER BE].

Polonius has in mind something much more Elizabethan than the New Age self-knowledge that the phrase now suggests. As Polonius sees it, borrowing money, loaning money, carousing with women of dubious character, and other intemperate pursuits are "false" to the self. By "false" Polonius seems to mean "disadvantageous" or "detrimental to your image"; by "true" he means "loyal to your own best interests." Take care of yourself first, he counsels, and that way you'll be in a position to take care of others. There is wisdom in the old man's warnings, of course; but he repeats orthodox platitudes with unwonted self-satisfaction. Polonius, who is deeply impressed with his wordliness, has perfected the arts of protecting his interests and of projecting seeming virtues, his method of being "true" to others. Never mind that this includes spying on Hamlet for King Claudius. Never mind, as well, that many of Polonius's haughty, if not trite, kernels of wisdom are now taken as Shakespeare's own wise pronouncements on living a proper life.

Tomorrow, and Tomorrow, and Tomorrow

MACBETH: To-morrow, and to-morrow, and to-morrow,
Creeps in this petty pace from day to day,
To the last syllable of recorded time;
And all our yesterdays have lighted fools
The way to dusty death. Out, out, brief candle!
Life's but a walking shadow, a poor player,
That struts and frets his hour upon the stage,
And then is heard no more. It is a tale
Told by an idiot, full of sound and fury,
Signifying nothing.

MACBETH   Act 5, scene 5, 19–28

After hearing that his wife has died, Macbeth takes stock of his own indifference to the event. Death—our return to dust —seems to him merely the last act of a very bad play, an idiot's tale full of bombast and melodrama ("sound and fury"), but without meaning ("signifying nothing"). Murdering King Duncan and seizing his throne in retrospect seem like scenes of a script Macbeth was never suited to play. The idea that "all the world's a stage" is occasionally very depressing to Shakespeare's heroes.

"To-morrow, and to-morrow, and to-morrow"—along with the other phrases culled from this lode of Bardisms—conveys the mechanical beat of time as it carries this poor player-king from scene to scene. "The last syllable of recorded time"— what Macbeth earlier called "the crack of doom" [*see* p. 25] —casts time as a sequence of words, as in a script; history becomes a dramatic record. If life is like a bad play, it is thus an illusion, a mere shadow cast by a "brief candle." The candle is perhaps the soul, and the prospects for Macbeth's are grim.

Too Much of a Good Thing

ORLANDO: Then love me, Rosalind.
ROSALIND: Yes, faith, will I, Fridays and Saturdays and all.
ORLANDO: And wilt thou have me?
ROSALIND: Ay, and twenty such.
ORLANDO: What sayest thou?
ROSALIND: Are you not good?
ORLANDO: I hope so.
ROSALIND: Why then, can one desire too much of a good thing?

AS YOU LIKE IT   Act 4, scene 1, 115–124

Of all the supposed bawdy puns in Shakespeare's work, this one's authentic. "Thing" was a common enough euphemism for either male or female genitalia, and the context here is certainly suggestive. Having used "too much of a good thing" in all innocence, you might find its original connotation embarrassing.

The indecency of this exchange may also surprise you once

you know that Rosalind and Orlando are the quintessential comic-romantic lovebirds, whose goodness and purity are never challenged. The reason Rosalind can speak this way is very complicated, but, briefly put, she's dessed up as a young man and, when she encounters her lover Orlando in the Forest of Arden, she decides to withhold her true identify from him. Yes, you say, but Orlando calls her "Rosalind" here. True, but that's because Rosalind, in the guise of the young man Ganymede, is "pretending" to be Rosalind so that she can train Orlando in courtship and teach him what women are "really" like. Through such play-acting, Rosalind may probe Orlando's intentions, and at the same time put his idealistic notions of courtly lovemaking to the test. She takes on the role of the comic dramatist, scripting a fantasy version of courtship in order to explore and expose its workings.

Touch of Nature

ULYSSES: Let not virtue seek
Remuneration for the thing it was;
For beauty, wit,
High birth, vigor of bone, desert in service,
Love, friendship, charity, are subjects all
To envious and calumnating Time.
One touch of nature makes the whole world kin,
That all with one consent praise new-born gawds,
Though they are made and moulded of things past,
And give to dust that is a little gilt
More laud than gilt o'erdusted.
                    TROILUS AND CRESSIDA   Act 3, scene 3, 169–179

Everyone agrees that "touch of nature" means "natural trait" —an essential characteristic that makes us all kin. Ulysses— author of the phrase—addresses it to his fellow Greek, the great warrior Achilles, who has recently been sitting out the Trojan War on account of wounded pride and a Trojan lover. Achilles wonders why prominent Greeks have been giving him the cold shoulder; Ulysses, hoping to goad his compatriot back into action, delivers an unflattering lecture on human nature. Our "touch of nature" isn't warmth or generosity or any other romantic ideal such as is the object of the phrase nowadays. Ulysses finds unanimity only in our prizing gaudy novelties ("new-born gawds"), anything with an unfamiliar, if superficial, sparkle. Achilles' past deeds, like beauty, wit, love, and so on, are subject to the ravages of time; it is our nature to forget faded glories. Our "touch of nature" is a short memory.

A Tower of Strength

KING RICHARD: Up with my tent! Here will I lie tonight—
But where to-morrow? Well, all's one for that.
Who hath descried the number of the traitors?
NORFOLK: Six or seven thousand is their utmost power.
KING RICHARD: Why, our battalia trebles that account!
Besides, the King's name is a tower of strength,
Which they upon the adverse faction want.

RICHARD THE THIRD Act 5, scene 3, 7–14

As the villainous King Richard III prepares to battle the forces of the virtuous Earl of Richmond (later Henry VII), he pitches his tent on Bosworth Field and banishes thoughts of possible defeat. His confidence, however, is shaken, despite the superiority of his forces—thrice as many as Henry's. At least, he assures himself, he has "the King's name," which ought to wield force no matter how brutal and corrupt the king. "The King's name is a tower of strength"—strong, tall, unassailable.

Richard's assertion perhaps derives from Proverbs 18:10— "The name of the Lord is a strong tower: the righteous runneth into it, and is safe." King Solomon's image makes more sense than King Richard's; it is easy to imagine the strength of a tower, but difficult to imagine a tower of strength. Richard could mean either "a strong tower" or "a tower built of strength," but in adopting the phrase we really lean toward the latter. We make the quality of a thing (the strength of a tower) into a freestanding material, as if it were like concrete.

Trippingly on the Tongue

HAMLET: Speak the speech, I pray you, as I pronounc'd it to you, trippingly on the tongue; but if you mouth it, as many of our players do, I had as lief the town-crier spoke my lines.

HAMLET Act 3, scene 2, 1–4

Having penned some lines for a play he hopes will pique the king's interest [see THE PLAY'S THE THING], Hamlet now assumes the role of director. He instructs the "players" (performers) on proper delivery, apparently fearing that they may smother his lines with the sort of bombast common on the stages of Shakespeare's London. Rather than "mouth" his speech—declaim it with the whole mouth—he would have them deliver it "trippingly on the tongue." "Trippingly" seems to mean "liltingly" or "nimbly," using only the delicate tongue rather than the full throat. This, Hamlet believes, will make for a more effective delivery, because it will be more like real speech.

Shakespeare coined the word "trippingly" in an earlier play, *A Midsummer Night's Dream*. There, Oberon the king of fairies commands all his elves and spirits to "Hop as light as bird from brier,/ And this ditty, after me,/ Sing, and dance it trippingly" (Act 5, scene 1). "Trippingly," as Oberon uses it, refers back to the light hopping of birds and is applied to the physical act of dancing. Hamlet attributes the adverb to the physical action of speech, but lends the word a more abstract meaning, imagining that the words themselves can "trip."

Uneasy Lies the Head that Wears a Crown

KING HENRY: Canst thou, O partial sleep, give thy repose
    To the wet sea-boy in an hour so rude,
    And in the calmest and most stillest night,
    With all appliances and means to boot,
    Deny it to a king? Then happy low, lie down!
    Uneasy lies the head that wears a crown.

    HENRY THE FOURTH, PART 2 Act 3, scene 1, 26–31

Tired, sick, guilty, and beset by rebellion, King Henry IV is feeling the weight of his crown. Why, even the "vile" of his realm, after hours of drudgery, can in their "loathsome beds" get a good night's sleep (lines 15–16), while he—a king!—cannot. The "wet sea-boy" perched high on a mast, amid wind and waves, nods off easily, while quiet nights on a royal couch bring no rest to poor King Henry. "Uneasy lies the head that wears a crown," he concludes, probably wishing that he hadn't seized the throne from the pathetic Richard II and then had him murdered.

Such belated regrets run in the family. Henry's abler son Hal, as King Henry V, pauses on the eve of the Battle of Agincourt to assess the "hard condition,/ Twin-born with greatness" that is kingship. "What infinite heart's ease/ Must kings neglect, that private men enjoy!" he wails (*Henry the Fifth*, Act 4, scene 1). Since neither he nor his father ever slept on the loathsome beds of vile private men, we wonder how they would know.

The Most Unkindest Cut of All

MARCUS ANTONIUS: For Brutus, as you know, was Caesar's angel.
Judge, O you gods, how dearly Caesar lov'd him!
This was the most unkindest cut of all;
For when the noble Caesar saw him stab,
Ingratitude, more strong than traitors' arms,
Quite vanquish'd him: then burst his mighty
heart. . . .

JULIUS CAESAR Act 3, scene 2, 181–186

Marc Antony is in the middle of his great speech on the assassination of Julius Caeser [*see* FRIENDS, ROMANS, COUNTRYMEN, LEND ME YOUR EARS]—which has very quickly turned into a character assassination of Brutus, a prominent republican, Caesar's friend and one of Caesar's murderers.

When Antony calls Brutus's stabbing of Caesar "the most unkindest cut of all," he is playing on two senses of "unkind" —"inhumane" and "unnatural." According to Antony, when

Brutus literally "cut" the loving Caesar, a bloody deed was compounded with ingratitude. It wasn't the wound that killed Caesar, says Antony, but Brutus's treachery.

Time has softened Antony's language: all that remain are a weaker sense of "unkind" and a less literal use of "cut." "Most unkindest," by the way, wasn't as ungrammatical in Shakespeare's day as it is in ours.

Unsex Me Here

LADY MACBETH: The raven himself is hoarse
That croaks the fatal entrance of Duncan
Under my battlements. Come, you spirits
That tend on mortal thoughts, unsex me here,
And fill me from the crown to the toe topful
Of direst cruelty!

MACBETH   Act 1, scene 5, 38–43

Lady Macbeth, upon receiving word that King Duncan of Scotland will be arriving that night, begins sharpening her talons. She isn't sure there's enough manhood to go around between herself and her husband, so she calls upon scheming spirits to "unsex me here." This is her vivid way of asking to be stripped of feminine weakness and invested with masculine resolve. She imagines herself as a vessel which may be emptied out and refilled "from the crown to the toe." One thing nobody, spirit or otherwise, has ever poured into her is "the milk of human kindness" [see p. 81].

The prefix un- is abnormally frequent in Macbeth. The protagonists constantly try to undo what is done, take back what is given, and cancel reality by appending negatives. All the powers of langauge, however, cannot cancel their unconscious conflicts, which manifest themselves in hallucinations and bad dreams.

Vale of Years

OTHELLO: Haply, for I am black,
And have not those soft parts of conversation
That chambers have, or for I am declin'd
Into the vale of years (yet that's not much),
She's gone. I am abus'd, and my relief
Must be to loathe her. O curse of marriage!

                              OTHELLO   Act 3, scene 3, 263–268

"Vale of years" shouldn't be confused with "vale of tears," although the echo is suggestive. A "vale" is a broad, flat valley; in the fifteenth century the word came to be a metaphor for the span of life between the peaks of birth and death—that is, life in this careworn world. "Vale of trouble and woe," "vale of weeping," "vale of misery," and "vale of tears" illustrate typical uses of the word before Shakespeare. Othello's phrase, however, seems intended in a more neutral sense; the "vale of years" is the broad, flat stretch of middle age beyond the slope of youth.

As Othello searches for reasons why his wife might be unfaithful to him—as his "honest" ensign Iago has all but convinced him—he thinks of his slow decline into the vale of years as one possibility. That he is dark-skinned, while his wife is white as alabaster, and that he thinks his "conversation" (discourse) coarse while hers is refined, are other possibilities, and they make Iago's accusations seem more likely. Iago has fabricated the whole scenario, knowing and playing on Othello's emotional and logical weaknesses.

Valiant Dust

LEONATO: Well, niece, I hope to see you one day fitted with a
    husband.
BEATRICE: Not till God make men of some other mettle than earth.
    Would it not grieve a woman to be overmaster'd with a piece of
    valiant dust? to make an account of her life to a clod of wayward
    marl? No, uncle, I'll none: Adam's sons are my brethren, and
    truly I hold it a sin to match in my kinred.

                     MUCH ADO ABOUT NOTHING   Act 2, scene 1, 57–65

One of the most attractive of Shakespeare's characters, Beatrice is also one of the most sharp-tongued. Like her male counterpart and eventual husband Benedick, she is "a profess'd tyrant" to the opposite sex, especially him. Here, her uncle

Leonato teasingly forecasts her eventually being "fitted" (furnished) with a spouse despite all her resistance. But Beatrice insists, only half jokingly, that it would be absurd and undignified to submit to a mere piece of "valiant dust."

Beatrice's use of "valiant" seems a little strange in this context, especially since she uses "wayward marl" (perverse clay) in parallel with "valiant dust." Today it sounds nobler than she intended. "Valiant" most likely means "sturdy" or "firm" here, a sense still current in Shakespeare's day. A man to Beatrice is merely dust molded into solid form. Besides, she quips, since we're all sons and daughters of Adam, marriage is inherently incestuous.

The Vasty Deep

GLENDOWER: I can call spirits from the vasty deep.
HOTSPUR: Why, so can I, or so can any man;
           But will they come when you do call for them?
GLENDOWER: Why, I can teach you, cousin, to command
           The devil.
HOTSPUR: And I can teach thee, coz, to shame the devil—
           By telling the truth. Tell truth and shame the devil.

                      HENRY THE FOURTH, PART 1   Act 3, scene 1, 52–58

The Welsh rebel Glendower parries with his "cousin" Henry Percy, a.k.a. "Hotspur," who is related to Glendower through marriage. These two have not been getting along, which has mostly to do with bad chemistry; each is addicted to a different kind of self-aggrandizement. As they plot against the sitting king, Henry IV, Hotspur mocks Glendower for his outrageous claims to control the devil and his spirits. While the hothead

Hotspur easily tolerates his own brags, he has no use for Glendower's shady mumbo-jumbo and tales of his prodigious birth.

Glendower insists that he can call spirits from the "vasty deep," that is, from vast depths, presumably the underworld. "Vasty" appears to be a form Shakespeare invented and that has been picked up in homage. The suffix -y serves no real purpose, except perhaps to add a convenient syllable to fill out a blank-verse line. The suffix may also be intended to smack of pretense, and thus to expose Glendower's self-satisfaction with his own phraseology.

Vaulting Ambition

MACBETH: I have no spur
To prick the sides of my intent, but only
Vaulting ambition, which o'erleaps itself,
And falls on th'other. . . .

MACBETH **Act 1, scene 7, 25–28**

Macbeth, trying to rationalize his impending murder of King Duncan, continues his great "If it were done" soliloquy [see THE BE-ALL AND THE END-ALL]. Unfortunately, as Macbeth has just explained to himself, there's no real justification for the crime—Duncan is his relative, a meek and pious man, a good king, and, furthermore, a guest at his castle. All this argues against so bloody a deed, which will appear unjustifiable to mortal and divine eyes alike.

Therefore, Macbeth has no "spur" to prick on his intent, which is likened to a wild steed—no motivation to inspire the murder. Continuing the horse metaphor, he can only draw on "vaulting ambition": an intense desire for power. His desire vaults even beyond its intrinsic limits ("o'erleaps itself") to land on "th'other" (the other side)—probably, to land somewhere unknown and beyond reason.

Compare this speech to its parallel in *Julius Caesar*—Brutus's soliloquy in which he rationalizes an assassination, but comes up with more probable motivations than Macbeth's [see THE SERPENT'S EGG].

We Came Crying Hither

LEAR: If thou wilt weep my fortunes, take my eyes.
        I know thee well enough, thy name is Gloucester;
        Thou must be patient; we came crying hither:
        Thou know'st, the first time that we smell the air
        We wawl and cry.

                              KING LEAR Act 4, scene 6, 176–180

Well after first meeting the Duke of Gloucester in this scene [see EVERY INCH A KING], the distracted Lear finally recognizes the old man, who is now blind. Lear offers the duke his own eyes in return for tears of pity—the king, like Gloucester, has been turned out by ungrateful children. Half ashamed of weeping, the king begs patience, pointing out with a non sequitur that we enter this cruel world crying, as is only natural. The infant's tears are an instinctive response to being wrenched from the womb into an uncaring universe. By likening his tears to a baby's, Lear begins to accept the humility of being, beyond his role as king, merely a man like any other.

What the Dickens

FORD: Where had you this pretty weathercock?
MRS. PAGE: I cannot tell what the dickens his name is my husband had him of. What do you call your knight's name, sirrah?
ROBIN: Sir John Falstaff.
FORD: Sir John Falstaff!

THE MERRY WIVES OF WINDSOR **Act 3, scene 2, 18–23**

"What the dickens!" is an oath referring, not to Charles, but to Satan. "Dickens" probably derives from a common English surname, or from "Dickin," the diminutive of "Dick." The reason it was substituted euphemistically for "devil" in the exclamation "What the devil!" probably has little to do with the behavior of some naughty Dickens, though. As with that other devilish substitute "deuce" ("What the deuce!"), the reason almost certainly lies in the sound and in the comic effect of the substitution itself. Many similar examples in Renaissance or modern English may be found—such as "marry" for "Mary" and "gosh" for "God."

Master Ford stumbles here into the middle of an elaborate

plot, concocted by his wife and Mrs. Page, to foil the lecherous advances of Sir John Falstaff. Ford sincerely believes that Falstaff will succeed in seducing his wife—if he hasn't already—and is therefore rather nervous about signs of collusion between Falstaff and his wife's comrade, Mrs. Page. That Falstaff's page Robin has become part of the Page household gives Master Ford some pause.

What's Done is Done

LADY MACBETH: How now, my lord, why do you keep alone,
Of sorriest fancies your companions making,
Using those thoughts which should indeed have died
With them they think on? Things without all remedy
Should be without regard: what's done, is done.

MACBETH Act 3, scene 2, 8–12

Lady Macbeth's soothing words are odd, to say the least, coming from a conspirator. She intends her blandishments to calm her husband, who's having more trouble than she forgetting that he murdered King Duncan. She means by "what's done, is done" exactly what we mean by it today—"there's no changing the past, so forget about it." Neither then nor now is the psychology of this advice very sophisticated, but the Lady isn't trying to be profound. She's merely trying to treat Macbeth's guilty hallucinations with the blandest possible palliative. When Lady Macbeth herself succumbs to guilty dreams, she will sing the same tune, but in a different key. Sleepwalking, as has become her wont, she mutters, as if to Macbeth, "What's done cannot be undone" (Act 5, scene 1, 68).

What's Past Is Prologue

ANTONIO: . . . Who's the next heir of Naples?
SEBASTIAN: Claribel.
ANTONIO: She that is Queen of Tunis; she that dwells
          Ten leagues beyond man's life; she that from Naples
          Can have no note, unless the sun were post—
          The Man i' th' Moon's too slow—till new-born chins
          Be rough and razorable; she that from whom
          We all were sea-swallow'd, though some cast again
          (And by that destiny) to perform an act
          Whereof what's past is prologue; what to come,
          In yours and my discharge.

THE TEMPEST   Act 2, scene 1, 245–254

The Tempest is full of theatrical metaphors, such as "what's past is prologue." The metaphor has been forgotten, and the phrase has devolved into distorted forms (like "past and prologue"). When Antonio tells Sebastian that they have the opportunity to "perform an act," he means Act I of their own heroic drama. What's happened so far (that is, "what's past") is the prologue to that play, and the script is henceforth in their hands (in their "discharge").

Prologues were common in Renaissance drama, though Shakespeare himself wrote few of them. The prologue usually set the scene and presented the givens of the play (this is the kind Antonio has in mind). "What's past is prologue," then, translates roughly as "What's already happened merely sets the scene for the *really* important stuff, which is the stuff our greatness will be made on."

The "act" Antonio proposes is that Sebastian murder his sleeping father, Alonso, King of Naples, and grab the crown. All of them are now "cast" on what they believe is a desert island, so Antonio presumes the crime could easily be covered up. Furthermore, Sebastian's elder sister Claribel is safely out of the way in Tunis; by the time any news of Alonso's death reached her there, newborn boys will have grown thick beards (their chins will be "rough and razorable").

The Whirligig of Time

FESTE: I was one, sir, in this enterlude—one Sir Topas, sir, but that's all one. "By the Lord, fool, I am not mad." But do you remember? "Madam, why laugh you at such a barren rascal? And you smile not, he's gagg'd." And thus the whirligig of time brings in his revenges.
MALVOLIO: I'll be reveng'd on the whole pack of you.

TWELFTH NIGHT Act 5, scene 1, 372–378

For being such a wet blanket, Malvolio has been duped and subsequently tormented by the revelers who congregate at the house of the lady Olivia [see AN IMPROBABLE FICTION]. Here, the clown Feste explains and excuses his role. Because Malvolio once complained to Olivia about the fool's foolishness, calling him a "barren rascal," Feste took on the role of the churchman Sir Topas, who is called in to "cure" Malvolio of his "madness"—the improbable behavior the revelers had driven him to. Feste's last word on the matter is "And thus the whirligig of time brings in his [its] revenges"; he means something like "you reap what you sow." "Whirligig"—originally a top or any rotary device—becomes in this phrase a metaphor for time, which whirls misdeeds back on the perpetrator [compare FULL CIRCLE]. "Whirligig" also lent a name to a con-

temporary machine for punishing thieves. This elaborate con-
traption seems to have resembled a large hamster's treadmill,
with a hatch in the cage which could be opened to drop the
victim into water.

Wild-Goose Chase

MERCUTIO: Come between us, good Benvolio, my wits faints.
ROMEO: Swits and spurs, swits and spurs, or I'll cry a match.
MERCUTIO: Nay, if our wits run the wild-goose chase, I am done; for
   thou hast more of the wild goose in one of thy wits than, I am
   sure, I have in my whole five.

ROMEO AND JULIET Act 2, scene 4, 67–73

Romeo and his voluble friend Mercutio have been trading off
a rapid fire of hilarious jokes, an exchange Mercutio likens to
a "wild-goose chase." Though this is the first record we have
of the phrase, the audience must have been familiar with the
real game, in which one horseman executed a series of difficult
maneuvers which others had to repeat in close succession.
(Thus Romeo's obscure "swits and spurs"—that is, "switch and

spurs," to control one's baffled steed.) The game was probably named after the flight pattern of a flock of wild geese, which obediently follows the often erratic lead of the head goose. Thus, perhaps, the latter-day sense of the phrase: the pursuit of an evasive leader evolved into the pursuit of an impossible or illusory goal.

Mercutio also refers to his "five wits." He doesn't mean the five senses, but rather the corresponding intellectual faculties: memory, imagination, fancy, common sense, and judgment.

On the Windy Side

CLAUDIO: [to Hero] Lady, as you are mine, I am yours; I give away
    myself for you and dote upon the exchange.
BEATRICE: Speak, cousin, or (if you cannot) stop his mouth with a kiss,
    and let not him speak neither.
DON PEDRO: In faith, lady, you have a merry heart.
BEATRICE: Yea, my lord, I thank it, poor fool, it keeps on the windy
    side of care.

MUCH ADO ABOUT NOTHING   Act 2, scene 1, 308–315

After Shakespeare's usual dose of anxiety and suspicion, the young and inexperienced Claudio is affianced to the young and inexperienced Hero. Hero's witty cousin Beatrice pokes a little fun at the timid bride-to-be, urging her either to say something or to "stop" Claudio's mouth—that is, kiss him. Pedro comments on Beatrice's merriness, which is noteworthy since she claims to despise the very idea of marriage [see VALIANT DUST]. Her heart, she replies, is like a "poor fool," who, to earn his keep, must keep on "the windy side of care." There is some disagreement as to where this image comes from, although critics and editors agree that "the windy side of care" means something like "out of care's way." A glum fool is an unemployed fool.

The phrase may derive, as the editor A. R. Humphries suggests, from a nautical image, so that to be on the "windy side" means to be to the windward of care and therefore to intercept the wind and steal it from care's sails. The *OED* guesses that the phrase means to be situated windward so as "not to be 'scented' and attacked" by care. Though both these derivations seem a little forced, I can suggest nothing better.

In a later comedy, *Twelfth Night,* Fabian approves a scurrilous and provocative letter that Sir Andrew Aguecheek has written to a supposed competitor in love. Sarcastically, Fabian tells Sir Andrew that "Still you keep o' th' windy side of the law" (Act 3, scene 4)—that is, he pulls back from the verge of slander, which might land him in court.

The Winter of Our Discontent

RICHARD: Now is the winter of our discontent
        Made glorious summer by this son of York;
        And all the clouds that low'r'd upon our house
        In the deep bosom of the ocean buried.

RICHARD THE THIRD   Act 1, scene 1, 1–4

Richard, the future king, opens his play not by protesting his discontent, but by celebrating an upturn in his family's fortunes. His brother Edward IV—they're sons of the Duke of York—has wrested the English crown from Henry VI and the Lancastrian house. So those who simply quote "Now is the winter of our discontent" are doing these lines a disservice, since the "now" actually modifies "made glorious" (i.e. "The winter is now made glorious summer"). To translate more loosely: "The oppression of our family, which made life like a long winter, has been turned to a summery contentedness now that my brother is king." Edward's emblem is the sun, and the radiance of his glory has dispelled the clouds that "lowered" (frowned) on the House of York. Richard's string of metaphors runs adrift, though, when he begins talking about burying clouds in the ocean.

But lest we get the idea that Richard couldn't be happier with the current state of affairs, he quickly begins grousing about Edward's decadent ways now that he's king. And from there he moves on to brooding over his own deformity—Richard was born hunchbacked and disfigured. In many respects, it's still winter for the restless Richard, who himself has ambitions for the throne. He attempts to bring on his own summer through manipulation, treachery, and murder, and, for a short time, he succeeds.

The Woman's Part

POSTHUMUS: Could I find out
The woman's part in me—for there's no motion
That tends to vice in man, but I affirm
It is the woman's part; be it lying, note it,
The woman's; flattering, hers; deceiving, hers;
Lust and rank thoughts, hers, hers; revenges, hers;
Ambitions, covetings, change of prides, disdain,
Nice longing, slanders, mutability,

All faults that name, nay, that hell knows,
Why, hers, in part or all; but rather, all;
For even to vice
They are not constant, but are changing still. . . .

CYMBELINE   Act 2, scene 5, 19–30

Posthumus Leonatus, the exiled husband of Princess Imogen of Britain, has been taken in by an Italian trickster, who claims to have made Posthumus a cuckold. More ready to believe in fabricated evidence than in his own wife's constancy, Posthumus flies into a raging soliloquy. Like Hamlet and Troilus before him, he extrapolates from one woman to all women; the infidelity of a single lover casts doubt even on one's own mother. He wants to rip out "the woman's part" in him—his mother's contribution—because it is the vicious part, the unfaithful part, the lying, flattering, deceiving, etc., part. His own weaknesses are not really his, insofar as he's a man; presumably even the vengeful rage he's in now is his mother's fault. For Posthumus, as for many a Shakespearean male, women are the essence of vacillation and inconstancy, plaguing true-hearted, constant men.

_____ Is the Word

LORENZO: Goodly Lord, what a wit-snapper are you! then bid them
  prepare dinner.
LAUNCELOT: That is done too, sir, only "cover" is the word.

THE MERCHANT OF VENICE   Act 3, scene 5, 49–52

JAILER: Come sir, are you ready for death?
POSTHUMUS: Over-roasted rather: ready long ago.

JAILER: Hanging is the word, sir. If you be ready for that, you are well cook'd.

CYMBELINE Act 5, scene 4, 151–154

Shakespeare uses some form of "_____ is the word" at least five times in his plays, and I've presented here the earliest and one of the latest occurrences. For the clown Launcelot, who's been put in charge of supervising a banquet, "cover" ("lay the table-cloths") is the word; for King Cymbeline's jailer, "hanging" is the word. Launcelot means something like "I'm only waiting for the command 'cover' "; the jailer uses the phrase in a sense slightly closer to ours. He too waits upon a command—"hang 'im"—but he also means "hanging is the business at hand; the word 'hanging' is the precise word for your situation."

That Shakespeare used this expression with some frequency has led certain scholars to assume that it's proverbial. On the other hand, Shakespeare may have invented it and then grown paternally fond of it. No one has yet turned up an earlier example in surviving writings.

Let the World Slip

SLY: Marry, I will, let them play it. Is not a comonty a Christmas gambold, or a tumbling-trick?

PAGE: No my good lord, it is more pleasing stuff.

SLY: What, household stuff?

PAGE: It is a kind of history.

SLY: Well, we'll see't. Come, madam wife, sit by my side, and let the world slip, we shall ne'er be younger.

THE TAMING OF THE SHREW Induction, scene 2, 137–144

When the tinker Christopher Sly passes out drunk, he's found by the local lord who whisks him home. This aristocrat, who's one real practical joker, comes up with the hilarious idea of convincing Sly that he's only *dreamed* he's a tinker, when he's in fact a nobleman. Employed in this deceit is the lord's page, who dresses up—just like boys in commercial theaters—as the noble Sly's attractive young wife. As part of Sly's "therapy," to aid in his recovery from a fifteen-year dream, traveling players are brought in to present a comedy: *The Taming of the Shrew.* Sly doesn't know what a "comonty" (his blunder for "comedy") is—perhaps, he guesses, a holiday gambol or an acrobatic trick. Assured that a comedy is a kind of "history" (narrative), Sly assents. "Let the world slip," he exclaims: let's forget the cares of everyday business, because we're not getting any younger and we ought to have our fun. (The play proves to be so much fun that Sly nods off now and again, before disappearing from the text altogether.)

"Let the world slip" echoes Sly's earlier "Let the world slide" (Induction, scene 1). Both are new variations on older phrases, which date back at least to the early fifteenth century. "Let the world pass" is the earliest recorded form, but the most popular before Shakespeare was "Let the world wag." As the similarly low-born plowman says in the 1529 play *Gentleness and Nobility,* "I will let the world wag and home will I go/ And drive my plough as I was wont to do." But where the plowman sees letting the world wag as a return to his routine, Sly sees letting the world slip as an escape from the everyday, and this is pretty much how we use the phrase today.

The World's Mine Oyster

FALSTAFF: I will not lend thee a penny.
PISTOL: Why then the world's mine oyster,
          Which I with sword will open.
FALSTAFF: Not a penny.

THE MERRY WIVES OF WINDSOR **Act 2, scene 2, 2–5**

If you boast that "The world's my oyster" nowadays, you're claiming that the world's riches are yours to leisurely pluck from the shell. The braggart ensign Pistol, however, utters the phrase as a sort of threat—of the aggressively bombastic kind he's known for. Sir John Falstaff, a braggart almost the equal of Pistol, refuses to lend him a penny; Pistol promises to use his sword, if not on Falstaff, then on other helpless victims, to pry open their purses. Pistol's thievish intentions have largely been forgotten, and "The world's my oyster" has become merely a conceited proclamation of opportunity.

Alas, Poor Yorick

FIRST CLOWN: A pestilence on him for a mad rogue! 'a pour'd a flagon
  of Rhenish on my head once. This same skull, sir, was, sir,
  Yorick's skull, the King's jester.
HAMLET: This? [*Takes the skull*]
FIRST CLOWN: E'en that.
HAMLET: Alas, poor Yorick! I knew him, Horatio, a fellow of infinite
  jest, of most excellent fancy. He hath bore me on his back a
  thousand times, and now how abhorr'd in my imagination it is!
  My gorge rises at it.

HAMLET   Act 5, scene 1, 179–188

As two clowns dig Opelia's grave [*see* CUDGEL THY BRAINS],
they unearth the skull of Yorick, court jester to the former
king. This king's son, Prince Hamlet, just happens to be stroll-
ing through the graveyard with his friend Horatio, and he joins
the first clown in a round of morbid jokes. Hamlet's spirits,
however, are dampened by the smelly skull, whose grim visage
belies the prince's vivid memories of the frolicsome rogue. In
his characteristically associative fashion, Hamlet takes the
sickening contrast between the Yorick he imagines and his
disgusting remains as a leaping-point into sweeping philosophical conclusions about the common fate—decay—of both
kings and court jesters.

"Alas, poor Yorick" has always been one of the most fondly
remembered lines from *Hamlet* (or misremembered lines—
Hamlet does *not* say "Alas, poor Yorick, I knew him well").
As early as 1760, in his novel *Tristram Shandy*, Laurence Sterne
introduced the parson Yorick, one of whose ancestors emi-
grated from Denmark to England to become the English king's
court jester. In fact, the narrator claims, "*Hamlet's Yorick*, in
our *Shakespear*, many of whose plays, you know, are founded
upon authenticated facts,—was certainly the very man."

"Household Words":

COMMON AND UNCOMMON WORDS COINED BY SHAKESPEARE

POLONIUS: What do you read, my lord?
HAMLET: Words, words, words.

HAMLET **Act 2, scene 2, 191–192**

It's always impossible to know who first coined a word—and not much easier to know who first wrote it down. But here's a partial list of the words for which Shakespeare is the first authority the *Oxford English Dictionary* could find. Some words predate the first citation in the *OED*, even in its second edition. In a few cases, Shakespeare was the first to have used the word in at least one of its modern senses; these words are marked with a bullet (•). All verbs are in the infinitive form—that is, the "to" form ("to belly," "to overstink," etc.). Where there might otherwise be confusion over the part of speech, I have spelled it out.

abstemious
Academe
accessible
accommodation (a variation of
   "accommodations")

addiction (Shakespeare meant
   "tendency")
admirable [earlier than *OED*]
aerial (Shakespeare meant "of
   the air")

airless
amazemen
anchovy
arch-villain
to arouse
assassination
auspicious
bachelorship ("bachelorhood")
to barber
barefaced
baseless
basta! (first use in English)
batty (Shakespeare meant "bat-like")

beachy ("beach-covered")
to bedabble
to bedazzle
bedroom (Shakespeare meant "room in bed")
to behowl
to belly ("to swell")
belongings
to bemad
to bemonster
to besmirch

to bet
to bethump
to bewhore
birthplace
black-faced
to blanket
bloodstained
bloodsucking
blusterer
bodikins ("little bodies")
boggler ("slow-poke"; "stickler")
bold-faced
bottled (Shakespeare meant "bottle-shaped")
braggartism
brisky
broomstaff ("broom-handle")
budger ("one who budges")
bullyrook ("pal")
bum-bailie (term of contempt for a bailiff)
bump (as a noun)
buzzer (Shakespeare meant "tattle-tale")
to cake
candle holder
to canopy
to castigate
• to cater (as "to purvey food")
catlike
to champion
to channel (Shakespeare meant "to form a channel")
characterless

- cheap (in the pejorative sense: "flimsy," "vulgar")
cheese-paring
chimney-top
choppy (Shakespeare meant "chapped")
churchlike
circumstantial
clodpoll ("blockhead")
cloyment
clyster pipe ("enema tube")
cold-blooded
coldhearted
compact (the noun: "agreement")
to comply
to compromise (Shakespeare meant "to agree")
consanguineous
control (the noun)
coppernose ("a kind of acne")
countless
courtship
- to cow (as "to intimidate")
to crank (Shakespeare meant "to reel about"—"to come cranking in" is his coinage)
critical
cross-gartered
cruelhearted
to cudgel
Dalmatian [earlier than OED]
to dapple
dauntless
dawn (the noun)

day's work
death's-head
defeat (the noun)
to denote
depository ("trustee")
to deracinate
dewdrop
dexterously (Shakespeare spelled it "dexteriously")
to discandy ("melt")
disgraceful (Shakespeare meant "unbecoming")
to dishearten
to dislocate
distasteful (Shakespeare meant "showing disgust")
distracted (Shakespeare meant "crazed")
distrustful
dog-weary
doit (a Dutch coin: "a pittance") [earlier than OED]
domineering
downstairs
drollery
droplet
dry-nurse
duteous
to dwindle
East Indies
to educate
to elbow
embrace (the noun)
employer
employment

to enclog ("to hinder")

enfranchisement (Shakespeare didn't have voting rights in mind)

engagement [earlier than *OED*]

to enmesh

enrapt

to ensnare

to enthrone

epileptic

equivocal

eventful

excitement (Shakespeare meant "incitement")

expedience

expertness

exposure

exsufflicate ("puffed up")

eyeball

eyebeam

eyedrop (Shakespeare meant "tear")

eyewink

fair-faced

fairyland

fanged

fantastico ("someone prone to fantasies")

fap ("intoxicated")

farmhouse

far-off

fashionable

fashionmonger [earlier than *OED*]

fathomless (Shakespeare meant "too huge to be encircled by one's arms")

fat-witted

featureless (Shakespeare meant "ugly")

fiendlike

to film (Shakespeare meant "to film over")

to fishify ("turn into fish")

fitful

fixture (Shakespeare meant "fixing" or "setting firmly in place")

flapdragon (a raisin soaked in brandy and set aflame)

fleer (as a noun: "sneer")

fleshment ("the excitement of a first success")

flirt-gill (a "floozy")

• flowery (as we use it to mean "full of florid expressions")

fly-bitten

footfall

foot landraker ("footpad")

foppish
foregone
fortune-teller
to forward ("to advance")
foster-nurse
foul-mouthed
fount
Franciscan
freezing (as an adjective)
fretful
frugal
fubbed off ("fobbed off")
full-grown [earlier than OED]
fullhearted
futurity
gallantry (Shakespeare meant "gallant people")
garden house
generous (Shakespeare meant "gentle," "noble," "fair")
gentlefolk
glow (as a noun)
to glutton
to gnarl
go-between
to gossip (Shakespeare meant "to make oneself at home like a gossip—that is, a kindred spirit or fast friend")
grass plot
gravel-blind ("almost stone-blind")
gray-eyed
green-eyed
grief-shot ("sorrow-stricken")

grime (as a noun)
to grovel
• gust (as "a wind-blast")
half-blooded
to hand (Shakespeare meant "to handle")
to happy ("to gladden")
heartsore
hedge-pig
hell-born
to hinge
hint (the noun)
hobnail (the noun)
hodge-pudding ("a pudding of various ingredients")
• homely (in the sense of "ugly")
honey-tongued
hornbook ("alphabet tablet")
hostile
hot-blooded
howl (the noun)
to humor
hunchbacked ["bunch-back'd" in earliest edition]
hurly ("commotion")
to hurry
idle-headed
ill-tempered
ill-used
impartial
to impede
implorator ("solicitor")
import (the noun: "importance," "significance")
inaudible

inauspicious

indirection

indistinguishable

inducement

informal (Shakespeare seems to have meant "unformed" or "irresolute")

to inhearse ("load into a hearse")

to inlay

to instate (Shakespeare, who spelled it "enstate," meant "to endow")

inventorially ("in detail")

investment (Shakespeare meant "a piece of clothing")

invitation

invulnerable

jaded (Shakespeare seems to have meant "contemptible")

juiced ("juicy")

keech ("solidified fat")

kickie-wickie (derogatory term for a wife)

kitchen-wench

lackluster

ladybird

lament

land-rat

to lapse

laughable

leaky

leapfrog

lewdster

loggerhead (Shakespeare meant "blockhead")

lonely (Shakespeare meant "lone")

long-legged

love letter

to lower (Shakespeare meant both "to frown, to threaten" and "to sink, to decline")

lustihood

lustrous

madcap (as an adjective)

madwoman [earlier than OED]

majestic

malignancy (Shakespeare meant "malign tendency")

manager

marketable

marriage bed

marybud ("bud of a marigold")

mewling ("whining, whimpering")

militarist (Shakespeare meant "soldier")

mimic (the noun)

misgiving (the noun: "uneasiness")

to misquote

mockable ("deserving ridicule")

money's worth ["money-worth" dates from the fourteenth century]

monumental

moonbeam
mortifying (the adjective)
motionless
mountaineer (Shakespeare
    meant "mountain-dweller")
to muddy
multipotent ("most mighty")
multitudinous
mutineer
nayword ("byword")
neglect (the noun)
to negotiate
never-ending [earlier than
    OED]
newsmonger
nimble-footed
noiseless
nonregardance ("disregard")
nook-shotten ("full of corners
    or angles")
to numb [earlier than OED]
obscene (Shakespeare meant
    "revolting")
ode
to offcap ("to doff one's cap")
offenseful ("sinful")
offenseless ("unoffending")
Olympian (Shakespeare meant
    "Olympic")
to operate
oppugnancy ("antagonism")
outbreak
to outcrafty ("to excel in craft";
    "outwit")

to outdare
to outfrown
to outgrow
to out-Herod ("to outdo Herod
    in bluster")
to outscold
to outsell (Shakespeare meant
    "to exceed in value")
to outstare
to outswear
to outsweeten ("to be sweeter
    than")
to out-talk
to out-villain
to outweigh
overblown (Shakespeare meant
    "blown over")
to overbulk ("to surpass in
    bulk")
overcredulous
overgrowth
to overpay
to overpower
to overrate
to over-red ("to redden over")
to overstink ("to stink more
    than")
overview (as a noun:
    Shakespeare meant
    "supervision")
pageantry
to palate (Shakespeare meant
    "to relish")
pale-faced

to pander

passado (a kind of sword-thrust)

paternal

pauser ("one who hesitates")

pebbled ("pebbly")

pedant (Shakespeare was referring to a schoolmaster)

pedantical

pendulous (Shakespeare meant "hanging over")

to perplex

perusal

to petition

pignut (a sort of tuber)

pious

please-man ("yes-man" or "parasite")

plumpy ("plump")

posture (Shakespeare seems to have meant something like "position" or "positioning") [earlier than OED]

pouncet-box ("small box for perfumes")

prayerbook [earlier than OED]

priceless

profitless

Promethean

protester (Shakespeare meant "one who affirms")

published (Shakespeare meant "commonly recognized")

puh! (an interjection signifying disgust and/or condescension)

to puke

puppy-dog

pushpin (Shakespeare was referring to a children's game)

on purpose

quarrelsome

in question (as in "the ____ in question")

radiance

to rant

rascally [earlier than OED]

rawboned ("very gaunt")

razorable ("fit to be shaved")

reclusive

refractory

reinforcement (Shakespeare meant "renewed force")

reliance

remorseless

reprieve (the noun)

resolve (the noun)

restoration [earlier than OED]

• restraint (as "reserve")

retirement

to reverb ("to re-echo")

revokement ("revocation")

revolting (Shakespeare meant "rebellious") [earlier than OED]

to reword (Shakespeare meant "re-echo" and "repeat")

ring carrier ("go-between")

ring-time ("time for exchanging rings")

to rival (Shakespeare meant "to compete")

roadway

roguery

rose-cheeked

rose-lipped

rug-headed ("shock-headed")

rumination

ruttish

sacrificial

sanctimonious

to sate

satisfying (as an adjective)

• savage (as "uncivilized")

savagery

schoolboy

scrimer ("a fencer")

scroyle ("wretch")

scrubbed (Shakespeare meant "stunted")

scuffle

seamy ("seamed") and seamy side ("under-side of a garment")

to secure (Shakespeare meant "obtain security")

self-abuse (Shakespeare meant "self-deception")

semblative ("resembling")

shipwrecked (Shakespeare spelled it "ship-wrackt")

shooting star

shudder (the noun)

silk stocking

silliness

to sire

skimble-skamble ("senseless")

skim milk [in quartos; "skim'd milk" in the Folio]

slugabed

to sneak

sneap ("snub"—as a noun and as a verb)

soft-hearted

spectacled

spilth ("something spilled")

spleenful

sportive

to squabble

stealthy

stillborn

to subcontract (Shakespeare meant "to remarry")

successful

suffocating (the adjective)

to sully

superscript (Shakespeare meant "address written on a letter")

superserviceable ("more serviceable than is necessary")

to supervise (Shakespeare meant "to peruse")

to swagger

tanling ("somone with a tan")

tardiness

time-honored
title page [earlier than *OED*]
tortive ("twisting")
to torture
traditional (Shakespeare meant
    "tradition-bound")
tranquil
transcendence
trippingly
unaccommodated
unappeased
to unbosom
unchanging
unclaimed
• uncomfortable (in the sense
    "disquieting")
to uncurl
to undervalue (Shakespeare
    meant "to judge as of lesser
    value")
to undress
unearthly
uneducated
to unfool
unfrequented
ungoverned
ungrown
to unhand (as in the phrase
    "unhand me!")
to unhappy
unhelpful
unhidden
unlicensed
unmitigated

unmusical
to unmuzzle
unpolluted
unpremeditated
unpublished (Shakespeare
    meant "undisclosed")
unquestionable (Shakespeare
    meant "impatient")
unquestioned
unreal
unrivaled
unscarred
unscratched
to unsex
unsolicited
unsullied
unswayed (Shakespeare meant
    "unused" and "ungoverned")
untutored
unvarnished
• unwillingness (in the sense
    "reluctance")
upstairs
useful
useless
valueless
varied (as an adjective)
varletry
vasty
vulnerable
watchdog
water drop
water fly
well-behaved

well-bred
well-educated
well-read
to widen (Shakespeare meant
  "to open wide")
wittolly ("contentedly a
  cuckold")

worn out (Shakespeare meant
  "dearly departed")
wry-necked ("crook-necked")
yelping (as an adjective)
zany (a clown's sidekick or a
  mocking mimic)

Faux Shakespeare:

PHRASES OFTEN MISATTRIBUTED
TO SHAKESPEARE

In *Julius Caesar* (1599), the conspirator Casca admits that a speech of Cicero's "was Greek to me" (Act 1, scene 2). Twenty-four years later the play was published in the Shakespeare First Folio, whence it passed into edition after edition of the Bard's works and ultimately into the hands of today's pedagogues. In many a classroom, incredulous seventeen-year-olds are now shown that, not only did the Greatest Author in the English Language write all those tedious speeches full of tortuous locutions, but he also invented all kinds of cool phrases that regular people use all the time. "It's Greek to me," some smart-aleck student might respond when asked to explain to the class "If th'assassination could trammel up the consequence," those quoting Shakespeare in his own defense.

Meanwhile, mountains of dust rise on George Gascoigne's *Supposes* (1575), a play no high school student and very few pedagogues have ever read, though Shakespeare himself almost certainly did. Anyway, pull your copy of *Supposes* off the shelf, and look at Act 1, scene 1; round about line 92 the confused nurse Balia admits that "This geare [business, plot] is Greeke to me."

After devoting most of a book to all the wonderful phrases that Shakespeare did in fact coin, I doubt it will detract from his glory to set the record straight as regards "*faux* Shakespeare" —lines commonly but mistakenly touted as Shakespeare originals. Just because the Bard was a regular phrase-coining machine doesn't mean he should hog the credit when the facts are against him. I admit that in most cases Shakespeare's usage is far better known than the original; but you will misrepresent the Bard, and risk making a fool of yourself, if you go around telling people that Shakespeare invented something that, in reality, the glover around the corner uttered once a week, without thinking anything of it.

Thus the following list of phrases sometimes laid at Shakespeare's door but which are (for better or or for worse) someone else's responsibility. Not that I'm casting stones; it's quite possible that a number of the phrases featured in this book were proverbial, and that someone might someday document earlier occurrences in the surviving literature. I merely report the current state of knowledge about familiar phrases that can be definitively shown *not* to be of Shakespeare's invention.

"ALL THAT GLISTERS IS NOT GOLD" reads a scroll placed in a golden casket, in *The Merchant of Venice* (Act 2, scene 7). "But all thing which that shineth as the gold, nis not gold, as that I have heard it told," says the Canon's Yeoman in Chaucer's *Canterbury Tales* (ca. 1386). Thomas Becon, in *Reliques of Rome* (1553), insists that "All is not gold that glistreth." In his Italian-English lexicon of 1578, John Florio points out that "All that glistreth is not gold." Not only isn't Shakespeare first, he doesn't even win a medal.

"AS SOUND AS A BELL," as Don Pedro puts it in *Much Ado about Nothing* (Act 3, scene 2), was also proverbial; it had already been used by, for example, Thomas Newton in a 1576 translation from the Latin: "They be people commonly healthy, and as sounde as a bell."

"BELL, BOOK AND CANDLE" were props in the medieval excommunication ceremony before they were invoked by the bastard Faulconbridge in *King John* (Act 3, scene 3). Faulconbridge may perhaps leave us with the first written record of this particular permutation of the three words, but the phrase "candle, book, and bell" shows up around 1300.

"TO KNIT ONE'S BROW" is a phrase sometimes thought to trace to *Henry the Sixth, Part 2* (Act 3, scene 1), but Chaucer also used it, in the *Knight's Tale:* "This Palamon gan nit his brows tweye [two]."

"COLD COMFORT" is uttered by both Grumio in *The Taming of the Shrew* (Act 4, scene 1) and King John in his own play (Act 5, scene 7). But "cold comfort" is also how translator Arthur Golding (whose version of Ovid Ezra Pound highly recommended) renders a phrase in Calvin's commentary on the Book of Psalms (translated in 1571).

"HE WILL GIVE THE DEVIL HIS DUE" says Prince Hal of Falstaff in *Henry the Fourth, Part 1*; but even as he says it he calls it a "proverb." John Lyly uses a version of the phrase in his vituperative pamphlet *Pappe with a Hatchet* (1589).

"THE DOG WILL HAVE HIS DAY" (*Hamlet*, Act 5, scene 1) was labeled a proverb as early as the 1520s. And Princess Elizabeth

—later Queen—is reported to have said in 1550 that "Notwithstanding as a dog hath a day. . . ."

"ELBOW ROOM," from *King John* (Act 5, scene 7), is traced back to 1540 by the *OED*.

"ET TU, BRUTE?" cries Julius Caesar as Brutus and company apply their knives (*Julius Caesar*, Act 3, scene 1, 77). Shakespeare probably borrowed these famous last words from tradition. But, surprisingly, they do not occur in print in this form until about four years before *Julius Caesar* was first produced, in *The True Tragedy of Richard Duke of York* (published 1595). This play is believed to be a "bad" (unreliable) quarto of Shakespeare's own *Henry the Sixth, Part 3* (1590–91).

"TO PLAY FAST AND LOOSE" is a phrase that appears both in *Love's Labor's Lost* and in *King John,* and is attributed to Shakespeare almost as often as "It's Greek to me." But the *OED* finds the phrase in 1557 as the title of an epigram in a popular miscellany (what we would now call an "anthology"). The phrase originally referred to a sleight-of-hand trick.

"MINE OWN FLESH AND BLOOD" shows up in six different Shakespeare plays, which is evidence enough that the phrase was already in common use; but it has also been definitively traced back to 1565 at the latest.

"TILL THE LAST GASP" appears in 1577 [*see* BREATHE ONE'S LAST].

"LAUGHING STOCK" (*The Merry Wives of Windsor,* Act 3, scene 1) is traced by the *OED* to 1533, and is also used in Sir Philip Sidney's *Apology for Poetry* (1581).

"NOTHING COMES AMISS, so money comes withal," jests Grumio in *The Taming of the Shrew* (Act 1, scene 2). We know that the expression was common from its cameo appearance in a letter, supposedly by one Robert Langham, written in the 1570s. Some scholars, however, wish to attribute this piece of work to Edward de Vere, 17th Earl of Oxford. Oxford is the current favorite of conspiracy theorists who argue that someone other than Shakespeare wrote Shakespeare's plays. So maybe "Shakespeare" coined the phrase after all.

"FOOL'S PARADISE" *should* have been Shakespeare's, but William Paston insisted in 1462 that "I wold not be in a folis paradyce." The phrase turns up in *Love's Labor's Lost* and *Romeo and Juliet*.

"IN A PICKLE" appears in *The Tempest* (Act 5, scene 1); a related form appears in *Antony and Cleopatra* (Act 2, scene 5). Thomas Tusser had advised, in 1573, that the husbandman "Reap barley with sickle, that lies in ill pickle." John Foxe (of the mammoth *Acts and Monuments*, a.k.a. "Foxe's Book of Martyrs") applied the homely metaphor in his 1585 sermon on Paul's second letter to the Corinthians: "In this pickle lieth man by nature, that is, all we that be Adam's children."

"OUT OF THE QUESTION" is sometimes given to Shakespeare because a related phrase, "out of question," was thought to originate in *Love's Labor's Lost*. The second edition of the *OED*, however, finds an identical use of "out of question" in 1586. Out of *the* question first appears around 1700.

"KISS THE ROD," which means "submit to one's master," is a phrase best remembered for its uses in Shakespeare's *The Two*

Gentlemen of Verona and *Richard the Second,* but it appears in Sir Philip Sidney's *Arcadia,* written in the 1580s and published around 1590.

"THE LONG AND THE SHORT OF IT"—or, as in Shakespeare, "the short and the long" (*The Merry Wives of Windsor,* Act 2, scene 1)—actually appeared at about the turn of the sixteenth century, according to the *OED.*

"THEREBY HANGS A TALE" (*The Taming of the Shrew,* Act 4, scene 1) was once thought to be the clown Grumio's punning distortion of the old "thereby lies a tale." (Tale/tail, get it?) But "hangs" was used by soldier and poet Thomas Churchyard in 1579.

"SET YOUR TEETH ON EDGE," which appears in *Henry the Fourth, Part 1* and *The Winter's Tale,* dates from at least the 1535 translation of Jeremiah 31:29: "The fathers have eaten a sour grape, and the childrens' teeth are set on edge."

"IT'S HIGH TIME," says Antipholus of Syracuse in *The Comedy of Errors* (Act 3, scene 2), but the phrase appears in the 1393 edition of Langland's *Piers Plowman* and is used in its current metaphorical sense by 1581.

"TELL TRUTH AND SHAME THE DEVIL," Hotspur mocks [*see* THE VASTY DEEP]. The phrase, which also appears in *The Merry Wives of Windsor,* dates from 1548.

"THE NAKED TRUTH" is that John Lyly used this phrase in his immensely popular *Euphues* (1578), a generation before its appearance in three of Shakespeare's plays and in "Sonnet 103."

"THE TRUTH WILL COME TO LIGHT" and "THE TRUTH WILL OUT"—both from *The Merchant of Venice*, Act 2, scene 2— are based on proverbs dating from at least the eleventh century. "Truth will out" appears in this form by 1439.

"THE WEAKER VESSEL," an unflattering phrase applied to females in three Shakespeare plays, is proverbial from 1576, and seems based on a verse from the first epistle of Peter 3:7, which reads, in the King James version (1611): "Likewise, ye husbands, dwell with them according to knowledge, giving honour unto the wife, as unto the weaker vessel. . . ."

"MAKE A VIRTUE OF NECESSITY," counsels one of the outlaws in *The Two Gentlemen of Verona* (Act 4, scene 1), but this is also Cressida's rationalization of her betrayal in Chaucer's *Troilus and Criseyde* (ca. 1374).

"THE WEAKEST GOES TO THE WALL," Capulet's servant Gregory explains in *Romeo and Juliet* (Act 1, scene 1)—meaning that women (the "weaker vessels," as another character calls them a few lines later), as well as children and the elderly, were politely allowed to walk on the "inside track" of a sidewalk and to thus avoid getting splattered or jostled by street traffic. The phrase dates to about 1550, and the sentiment dates from about 1500.

"SITS THE WIND IN THAT CORNER?" asks Benedick in *Much Ado about Nothing*, and he was once thought to be mutating the older phrase "Sits the wind in that door?" But the second edition of the *OED* has found an earlier use of "corner," from 1562.

"SOMETHING IN THE WIND" there may be, but it isn't blowing from *The Comedy of Errors* (Act 3, scene 1); the phrase dates from 1571.

"I HAVE NOT SLEPT ONE WINK," complains Pisanio in *Cymbeline* (Act 3, scene 4). The phrase goes back to at least the fourteenth century.

Good Enough to Call Your Own:

TITLES BORROWED FROM SHAKESPEARE

The better part of this book has been devoted to Shakespeare's influence on our everyday speech. Now we turn to more self-conscious attempts to be catchy or literary or profound or commercial—sometimes all at once. Authors of all kinds have, like everyone else, turned to the Bard in a pinch; but sometimes they end up quoting him just because his language has so thoroughly permeated both written and spoken English that we almost *breathe* Shakespeare.

It's quite natural for catchy phrases to turn themselves into titles somewhere along the line—Shakespeare himself capitalized on few, including "all's well that ends well" and "much ado about nothing." The literary wheel has come full circle (**King Lear**) as Shakespeare's works have gradually become a vast public domain of catch phrases and poetic profundities. Indeed, why cudgel thy brains (**Hamlet**) when a time-tested title is ready to hand? From headlines to best-sellers to corporate reports, no written matter seems safe from a Shakespearean reference, intentional or otherwise.

I had originally hoped to provide a list of all the book titles pilfered from the Bard. As it turns out, only a madman would try to exhaustively catalogue such a list; this madman gave up after about five hundred of them. A true embarrassment of riches; if I needed any convincing not to call this book *Dressing Old Words New* ("**Sonnet 76**") or *Caviar to the General* (**Hamlet**), that did it. So I borrowed from Cole Porter instead, whose song "Brush Up Your Shakespeare" is the showstopper of the 1948 musical *Kiss Me Kate*. (But there's no escape: the title of the musical is itself a quotation from the play it adapts: **The Taming of the Shrew**.)

O, How the Bard Becomes It

Borrowing leads to more borrowings. Referring to the Bard is like eating potato chips: once you start, it's hard to stop. In this regard, Aldous Huxley ranks as one of the biggest gluttons; he dipped his hand into Shakespeare's bag at least seven times. Huxley could compass both the most patent of thefts (like 1922's *Mortal Coils*, from **Hamlet**) and the most furtive (like 1944's *Time Must Have a Stop*, from **Henry the Fourth, Part 1**).

Of course, Shakespeare loses nothing by it—in fact, he profits. Miranda's naive exclamation "O brave new world!" (**The Tempest**) didn't often leap off anyone's tongue until Huxley transformed it into the standard epithet for technological dystopia with his 1932 novel *Brave New World*. The success of this grim volume prompted the already all-too-willing Huxley to appropriate the line once again—for *Brave New World Revisited* (1958)—but by then he'd made the phrase his own.

Yet once a second generation of borrowers moved in on Huxley's territory, even the moderate initiative involved in appropriating "brave new world" straight out of **The Tempest** dissipated into reflex, if not into parody. Witness Robert Cooke's relatively early rerun, *Improving on Nature: The Brave New World of Genetic Engineering* (1977) and Grant Fjermedal's more recent, and more hair-raising, *The Tomorrow Makers: A Brave New World of Living Brain Machines* (1986). Although these latter-day Cassandras probably had Huxley's books foremost in mind, we brushed-up readers are prepared to remit a royalty to the Swan of Avon.

Of course, most authors who have swiped a few telling words from the Bard had already brushed up their Shakespeare thoroughly and wanted their readers to know it. D. H. Lawrence, for example, resorts to one of the most obvious of scenes for the short-story title "This Mortal Coil" (from **Hamlet**). Ingmar Bergman likewise goes where the action is—**Julius Caesar**— to title his film about a trapeze artist *The Serpent's Egg* (1977). Anyone who would call a book O *How the Wheel Becomes It* (Anthony Powell, 1983—from **Hamlet**) or a story "Mortality and Mercy in Vienna" (Thomas Pynchon, 1959—from **Measure for Measure**) assumes, perhaps too charitably, that everyone will recognize the Shakespearean provenance. And in a typical move, Valdimir Nabokov coyly plundered one of Shakespeare's least-read plays, **Timon of Athens**, for the title *Pale Fire* (1962)—perhaps to prove that he was more brushed-up than thou.

The list of writers who turned to Shakespeare for help reads like a literary honor roll. It's hard to know exactly what Charles Dickens had in mind when he called his weekly journal *Household Words* (published from 1850 to 1859), but the phrase seems to originate in Shakespeare's **Henry the Fifth**. Nonstop Victorian novelist Mary Elizabeth Braddon, author of *Lady Audley's Secret*, derived the title of her *Taken at the Flood* (no date) from Cassius's famous speech in **Julius Caesar** (Agatha Christie caught the same wave in 1948); Frederick Forsyth casts his lot with Cassius's nemesis Marc Antony when he calls down *The Dogs of War* (1974). David Halberstam quotes Antony's fellow-in-arms and future nemesis Octavius with *The Noblest Roman* (1961). Ogden Nash resorted to **Hamlet** for *The Primrose Path* (1935), borrowing the line from Ophelia. Echoing one of Prince Hamlet's more famous speeches, Archibald Macdonnell exclaims *How Like an Angel* (1935), and Rex Stout replies *How Like a God* (1929).

Joyce Carol Oates imagines Marc Antony's *New Heaven, New Earth* (1974, from **Antony and Cleopatra**); she forgets Godfrey W. Mathews's reminder that there are *More Things in Heaven and Earth, Horatio* (1934, from **Hamlet**). John Steinbeck turned to **Richard the Third** for *The Winter of Our Discontent* (1961); Dorothy Parker found *Not So Deep as a Well* (1936) in **Romeo and Juliet**, the same play Ford Madox Ford plumbed for *It Was the Nightingale* (1933). For his collection of essays W. H. Auden looked to Shakespeare's pessimistic "**Sonnet 111**" for the title *The Dyer's Hand* (1962).

The majority of Bard-pillagers—including the fifteen authors I found who called their books *What's in a Name?*—welcome the literary association. In other cases, I have some doubts. If twenty-six writers, including at least six poets, proudly name their offspring *Full Circle*, chances are that more than a few are oblivious to the origin of the phrase in **King Lear**. Of course, no one could have had originality chiefly in mind when they hit upon *Full Circle* anyway. Sir Edward Elgar must have been mulling over **Othello** when he composed "Pomp and Circumstance" in 1901, and Noel Coward, too, when he bestowed that title on his novel (1960). But how about Dorothea Gerard (1908), or Elisabeth duchesse de

Clermont-Tonnere (1929)? Did they advert to the Moor's tragedy, or Elgar's melody?

To Guard a Title that Was Rich Before

One glimpses an almost Darwinian pattern in the evolution of some Shakespearean titles—the daring initial appropriation is gradually, through the generations, domesticated as a distinct species. Perhaps C. K. Scott Moncrieff should have seen this coming when he took a line from "**Sonnet 30**" for his 1922 translation of Marcel Proust's *À la recherche du temps perdu*. *Remembrance of Things Past* has cozily settled into its niche as the instantly literary title for sentimental commemorative volumes and nostalgic memoirs—by, for example, John Howard (1925), Sir Henry Studdy Theobald (1935), and, in these more unsentimental times, F. F. Bruce (1980). We shouldn't forget to mention New Zealand's contribution to the genre, *Remembrance of Things Past: Solway College Golden Jubilee, 1966*. A long ways from Marcel's alma mater. As with Huxley, the credit goes neither to Moncrieff nor Shakespeare; but without that sonnet, we would be reading "In Search of Lost Time" and Proust would no doubt be even less widely read than he is now.

Every editorial page editor owes Shakespeare thanks for coining "What's past is prologue" (**The Tempest**)—"Past and prologue," for short. But so do institutions, who, if they could be said to have a favorite line, go for this one all the time. If I were a corporation poised at a historic juncture, I'd use it too. Mills College, in Oakland, California, seems to be the pioneer here, having published in 1951 its self-celebrating *"What's Past Is Prologue": 1852–1952, a Century of Education*. The quotation marks around the borrowing indicate a level of self-awareness and candor that was to disappear as quickly from the species as it evolved. When the American Association of Social Workers published its tome *What's Past Is Prologue* in 1955, the phrase had ceased to be a direct quotation and had become instead a kind of institutionalized formula. The American Civil Liberties Union briefly reverted back to quotation with its *Constitutional Liberty: "The Past Is Prologue"* (1958), but the use of quotation marks around a misquotation perhaps served as a negative example for posterity. Thus the unregenerate misquotation of *The Past Is Prologue . . . Human Welfare in the Next Half Century* (1964), a report sponsored by the American Federation for the Blind. Doyce B. Nunis, Jr., adopts the phrase to lend a cultured air to his *Past Is Prologue: A Centennial Portrait of Pacific Mutual Life Insurance Company* (1968), and he's joined by Wilfred A. Clarke in his *History of the Bank of Mexico: The Past Is Prologue* (1972). The centennial/semicentennial theme has by this point become inevitable, and the U.S. Highway Research Board follows suit in *Past and Prologue: The First Fifty Years* (1972), a title illustrating the final mutation of the phrase into the form we know from today's editorial pages.

Some Are Born Great, Some Achieve Greatness, and Some Have Greatness Thrust upon Them

Shakespeare is prime hunting ground for memoirists, who perhaps hope to register their names in the same immortal rolls as Hamlet and Macbeth. Douglas Fairbanks, Jr., looks back on *The Salad Days* (1988, from **Antony and Cleopatra**), as does Françoise Sagan (1984, English title). "One man in his time" (*As You Like It*) is particularly popular among biographers and autobiographers, who include Maud Skinner (1938), Nikolai

Borodin (1955), Serge Oblensky (1958), Phyllis Lean (1964), Alick West (1969), Marjorie Bishop (1979), and G. B. Harrison (1985). And if you're writing a flattering portrait of a monarch, what title could be more convenient than *Every Inch a King,* borrowed from **King Lear**? Princess Pilar of Bavaria and Major Desmond Chapman-Huston teamed up in 1932 to bestow this epithet upon King Alfonso XIII of Spain. Sergio Correa da Costa (or rather, his translator) was unembarrassed to apply the same title to his 1950 biography of the equally incomparable Dom Pedro I, first emperor of Brazil. King Hussein of Jordan shunned this company, opting instead to title his English-language reflections *Uneasy Lies the Head* (1962), perhaps thinking the weary Henry IV a more apt model than the insane Lear.

Whoever Herbert Chauncy was, we know from the biography by Sir Arthur Hallam Elton (Baronet) that he was *Herbert Chauncey: A Man More Sinned Against than Sinning* (1860, from **King Lear**). Roy Struben reports that an obscure relative was *Taken at the Flood* (1968, from **Julius Caesar**), also the title of another biography by John Gunther (1960). Sir John Rothstein set forth his life under the title *Summer's Lease* (1965, from "**Sonnet 18**"). For his own memoirs, Vincent Massey resorted to the by-then-familiar *What's Past is Prologue* (1963).

Critics and biographers who specialize in Tortured Artist figures instinctively turn to **Hamlet,** and home in on Polonius's assessment of the prince's ranting: "Though this be madness, yet there is method in't" (Act 2, scene 1). It turns out that almost exactly the same could be applied to numerous latter-day literary figures—witness Harvey Eagleson's "Gertrude Stein: Method in Madness" (1936), Edward Butscher's *Silvia Plath, Method and Madness* (1976), Roger S. Platizky's *A Blueprint of His Dissent: Madness and Method in Tennyson's Poetry*

(1989), and, with an interesting twist, Carol Becker's *Edgar Allan Poe: The Madness of the Method* (1975).

But writers aren't the only ones beset by schizoid tendencies; it's only just that, since Shakespeare was an actor and producer as well as a dramatic poet, actors and producers should get to share in Hamlet's condition. Dick Atkins first ventured this observation in *Method to the Madness: Hollywood Explained* (1975), and he was echoed by Maurice Yacowar, in *Method in Madness: The Art of Mel Brooks* (1981). Foster Hirsch shuns Hollywood to give "real" actors their due in *A Method to their Madness: A History of the Actors Studio* (1984). Those crazy artists!

Thankfully, not all creative minds are driven to despair. Other authors rush in to assure us that some famous literary figures were real family men and women. Leonard and Virginia Woolf, for example, made for *A Marriage of True Minds,* or so we are told by George Spater and Ian Parsons (1977, from **"Sonnet 116"**). N. Brysson Morrison presents *True Minds: The Marriage of Thomas and Jane Carlyle* (1974).

One Title in Its Time Plays Many Parts

Leaving the fertile field of literary madness, method, and marriage to others, some authors prefer to follow in Shakespeare's dramaturgical footsteps, and they want us to know with whom they associate themselves. In this genre falls the earliest instance of a Shakespearean title I could find: playwright Isaac Jackman's *All the World's a Stage* (1777, from **As You Like It**). Another eighteenth century testament to the Bard's long shadow is Frederick Reynolds's play *Fortune's Fool* (1796, from **Romeo and Juliet**). A certain Benjamin Webster staged his *One Touch of Nature* (from **Troilus and Cressida**) sometime in the nineteenth century, and George Brookes's own *All the World's a Stage* may also date from this era. We may more precisely place Thomas J. Williams's play *Cruel to be Kind* (1850, from **Hamlet**).

(Hamlet's dubious apology to his mother was picked up 128 years later by pop tunesmith Nick Lowe, whose "Cruel to be Kind" turned up as the flip-side of the single "Little Hitler." Another late-seventies rock act, Blondie, also plumbed Shakespeare for the punning title of their recent greatest-hits package, *Once More into the Bleach* [1989]—from Henry V's "Once more unto the breach.")

Upton Sinclair wrote a little-known play called *A Giant's Strength* (from **Measure for Measure**) in 1948; that same year, Florence Ryerson and Colin Clements staged *Strange Bedfellows* (from **The Tempest**), just as the original version of *Kiss Me Kate* was being written. The fifties seem to have been a dead time for Shakespeare-inspired play titles, but there was a revival of the fad in the 1960s, which saw the production of the musical *Salad Days* by Julian Slade and Dorothy Reynolds (1961, from **Antony and Cleopatra**), Louis D'Alton's *Lovers' Meeting* (1963, from **Twelfth Night**), and, most famous of all, Tom Stoppard's *Rosencrantz and Guildenstern are Dead* (1967, from **Hamlet**).

Time's Thievish Progress to Eternity

Writers looking for that inspiring touch of the grandiose and the ominous often bestir themselves no further than the nearest Shakespeare tragedy. Duncan Williams didn't have to look far for his *To Be or Not to Be: A Question of Survival* (1974). Marcia Millman needed a bloodier image for her *The Unkindest Cut: Life in the Backrooms of Medicine* (1978, from **Julius Cae-**

sar). ABC television sent chills up and down our spines with their **Macbeth**-inspired exposé, "Asbestos: The Way to Dusty Death" (*The Wide World of Learning*, 1978). H. C. Witwer, on the other hand, cleverly reworks Othello's last words while rescuing a cool-headed heroine from the jaws of terror in *Love and Learn: The Story of a Telephone Girl Who Loved Not Too Well but Wisely* (1924).

Perhaps most theftworthy of all is Macbeth's great speech from Act 5, scene 5 [*see* TOMORROW, AND TOMORROW, AND TOMORROW]. William Faulkner quotes this bleak little passage with the title of his well-known 1929 novel *The Sound and the Fury*. Though he was actually beaten to the punch by James Henle, who published *Sound and Fury* in 1924, Faulkner infused new vigor into the dismemberment of Macbeth's speech. *Sound and Fury* itself continued to be popular—Jackson Wright (1938), Francis Chase, Jr. (1942), Maurice Gorham (1948), Richard Collier (1963), the composer Jean Britton (1973), and Warner Troyer (1980) all used some version of the phrase. The line continues to nobly serve as the title of *Esquire* magazine's monthly letters-to-the-editor column.

From other lines in the same speech, we have numerous versions of *Tomorrow and Tomorrow*, and two books (including one by the unstoppable Huxley) which go the whole way: *Tomorrow and Tomorrow and Tomorrow*. *This Petty Pace* was wittily appropriated by the artist Mary Petty for her 1945 collection of drawings. Like *Tomorrow and Tomorrow*, the title *All Our Yesterdays* seems to be popular in science fiction circles, probably because of the *Star Trek* episode of that title. Jean Lissette Aroeste in fact adapted the popular teledrama as *All Our Yesterdays: A Star Trek Fotonovel* in 1978; John Peel caught on to the nostalgia in 1985 with his *All Our Yesterdays: The Star Trek Files*. Frank and Arthur Woodford lodge an entry with what may or may not be a work of science fiction, *All Our Yesterdays: A Brief History of Detroit* (1969).

Alastair MacLean plumbed Macbeth's speech for *The Way to Dusty Death* (1973), though his novel has nothing to do with asbestos. We've found two other authors besides Huxley who lighted on *Brief Candles;* three have availed themselves of the proximate *Walking Shadows.* Rose Macaulay wrote a tale, but not *Told by an Idiot,* in 1923. Malcolm Evans published *Signifying Nothing* in 1986 and was echoed a year later by Brian Rotman with *Signifying Nothing: The Semiotics of Zero.*

Besides *All Our Yesterdays* and *Tomorrow and Tomorrow,* a few other lines have lent themselves to science fiction. Ray Bradbury's *Something Wicked This Way Comes* (1962, also from **Macbeth**) may be the most famous, but Philip Dick's *Time out of Joint* (1959, from **Hamlet**) got there first. Scientists proper have not ignored the Swan of Avon, as demonstrated by James D. Ray, Jr., with his *What a Piece of Work Is Man: Introductory Readings in Biology* (1971, from **Hamlet**), and by Zdenek Jan Vaclavik's gripping *The Method in the Madness: A Unitary Neuro-Physiological Theory of Neurosis and Psychosis* (1961). Scholars of a popular pseudoscience edited a collection with the interest-piquing title *Economics: Myth, Method, or Madness?* (1971), if just to show that artists and neuro-physiologists have no corner on that market.

How Every Fool Can Play upon the Word

Every field, it seems, has its literary-minded advocates and detractors. Etiquette is no exception, as someone known only as "the Lounger in Society" manifested by publishing a guide-book called, naturally enough, *The Glass of Fashion* (1881, from **Hamlet**). Two of Shakespeare's most famous loungers have inspired festive-sounding publications. W. S. Maugham visits Sir Toby Belch in **Twelfth Night** for *Cakes and Ale* (1930). The obscure Herman Fetzer takes on the guise of another gastronome and writes *Pippins and Cheese* (1960, from **The Merry Wives of Windsor**) under the pseudonym "Jake Falstaff."

If you're thinking of inviting Toby or Jake over for a dinner party, you might want to have a few useful culinary guides on hand: Greta Hilb's *For Goodness Sake!* (1964, from **Henry the Eighth**), Alice H. Regis's *Cakes and Ale: The Ultimate Food Glossary* (1988, from **Twelfth Night**), and The San Diego, California, All Saints Church's *Sweets for the Sweet Tooth* (no date, from **Hamlet**).

If, on the other hand, you find yourself at a professional establishment, you might want to investigate the sociology of interactions between customers and the hired help, as analyzed in William R. Scott's *The Itching Palm: A Study of the Habit of Tipping in America* (1916, from **Julius Caesar**).

As in the social realm, writers concerned with politics have benefited from having Shakespeare's plays at hand in a pinch. When the Inns of Court Conservative and Unionist Society published its perhaps not intrinsically gripping ruminations on the state of labor, it turned to **Measure for Measure** for the title *A Giant's Strength: Some Thoughts on the Constitutional and Legal Position of the Trade Unions in England* (1958). Gertrude Stein, Mel Brooks, neuro-physiology, and economics have a companion in one nation-state, as John Kane-Berman describes it in *South Africa: The Method in the Madness* (1978). South Africa is not alone among nations in being honored (or dishonored) by association with the Bard; Mabel Segun adopts Marc Antony's deathless words for her *Friends, Nigerians, Countrymen* (1977, from **Julius Caesar**), and she is joined by

Hampton Howard in his recent *Friends, Russians, Countrymen* (1988).

Thou Com'st in Such a Questionable Shape

Speaking of Russia, Yuri Glazov poses a vexing question indeed in his *To Be or Not to Be in the Party: Communist Party Membership in the USSR* (also 1988). The same passage in **Hamlet** lept to the mind of the translator of Hans Christian Andersen's *To Be or Not to Be?* (translated 1857). *To Be or Not to Be a Jew* ponders Milton Steinberg (1950), but much more crucial is Claudia de Lys's query *To Be or Not to Be a Virgin* (1960)—*that* is the question.

Kill All the Lawyers? asks Sloan Bashinsky in a study subtitled *A Client's Guide to Hiring, Firing, Using and Suing Lawyers* (1986, from **Henry the Sixth, Part 2**). The subtitle already answers the question, and the formula is repeated by Peter Bragdon. "What's in a Name?" he inquires in the December 19, 1987, issue of *Congressional Quarterly Weekly Report;* "For Consultants, Much Cash" (from **Romeo and Juliet**). Less easily solved is James R. Carroll's poser, "Wherefore Art Thou, Jerry Brown?" (in *California Journal,* Nov. 1985)—for now, at least, he is reportedly in charge of the California Democratic party. The organization OMB Watch, which keeps its eye on the federal Office of Mangagement and Budget, doesn't stop to ask questions, but flatly declares *FY 89 Budget: The Stuff Dreams Are Made Of* (1988, misquoting **The Tempest**).

All Thy Other Titles Thou Hast Given Away

If you happen to be keeping score, Aldous Huxley emerges from this match the champ. The seven swipes I've been able to verify include *Mortal Coils* (1922, from **Hamlet**), *Brief Candles* (1930, from **Macbeth**), *Brave New World* (1932, from **The Tempest**), *Time Must Have a Stop* (1944, from **Henry the Fourth, Part 1**), *Ape and Essence* (1948, from **Measure for Measure**), *Tomorrow and Tomorrow and Tomorrow* (1958, from **Macbeth**), and *Brave New World Revisited* (also 1958). Left in the dust are William Dean Howells (score: 4) and the only other serious contender, the Nietzchean literary critic G. Wilson Knight (score: 5, further research pending). Though I continue to enumerate, log, and list, these three are nevertheless safely dead: the field is now wide open for any and all contenders. Pass the chips—the fun is just beginning.

Index of Words and Phrases

Index of Characters by Play